THE HARROWSMITH
Northern · Perennials
Handbook
BY PATRICK LIMA

CAMDEN HOUSE

ISBN 0-944475-04-3

Library of Congress Catalogue Card Number: 88-70640

Front Cover: *Peonies in the Larkwhistle Garden. Photograph by John Scanlan.*
Back Cover: *The Larkwhistle Garden in June. Photograph by John Scanlan.*

Designed by Pamela Orr

Printed in the U.S.A. by Boyd Printing Co. Inc. for
Camden House Publishing Inc.
The Creamery
Charlotte, Vermont 05445

Contents

Daylily

Perennial Pleasures

Three seasons of color for northern gardeners

Orange Lily

CHAPTER 1

When spring arrives," a friend responded after I asked her why she plants perennials, "three-quarters of my gardening work is already done. Many of the decisions about what goes where have been made. There's always something happening in a perennial bed: new plants flowering as others fade, a specially planned picture coming to life. It's exciting to watch the progress of perennials."

In the widest sense, a perennial is any

Corn Poppy

plant that lives from one season to the next, repeating each year the process of leafing out, flowering and seeding. (In contrast, annuals such as marigolds and nasturtiums accomplish all they have to do in one season. Once they have matured and dispersed seeds, they die.) Perennial plants intended to keep a northern garden colorful from year to year must also be hardy, that is, capable of surviving a full-blown northern winter. All of the plants discussed in this book, except for a few disappointments duly noted, have endured several winters here at Larkwhistle, our garden and home in central Ontario, where temperatures can drop to minus 40 degrees for short periods. However, a heavy snow cover, the very best protection for plant roots, invariably insulates our ground. Readers in areas where winters are either cold and dry or unpredictable in temperature and precipitation may have a different tale to tell about some of the perennials that we find successful.

The dependable snow has encouraged us to fill our garden with plants that hibernate underground for part of the year. To "hardy" and "perennial," therefore, as descriptions of most of our plants, I must add "herbaceous," a term that defines a plant's stems and leaves as soft and sappy, unlike the hard, woody, more or less permanent framework of shrubs and trees. The foliage and stems of many herbaceous plants die back to ground level over winter, while the roots remain dormant but alive, to sprout a fresh sheaf of greenery and a new crop of flowers each season. But not all perennials retreat for the cold months; pinks, candytuft, creeping phlox, arabis and other brave mountain plants keep their leaves year-round. These are hardy evergreen, or "evergray," herbaceous perennials. Throughout the text, when I use the word "perennial," the more exact term "hardy herbaceous perennial" is implied.

Hardy plants of one kind or another can bring color and beauty to every corner of a garden, but success is more likely to attend gardeners who know their plants. In the chapters that follow, I will make the introductions. After that, guided tours through other gardens—especially at times when your own lacks color—will always be instructive, as will strolls around botanical gardens and trips to local nurseries. Wherever you go, take note of plants that not only appeal to you but also appear to be thriving in an environment similar to your own.

The Environment

The first step, then, toward a thriving flower garden is an assessment of that environment. Take a look at your own situation, and indulge in flights of fancy tempered by a realistic appraisal of the site. Before you select plants, it is important to determine if their once-and-future home will suit them. Questions to ask are:

• How long does the sun shine here each day and for what part of the day? Sun-loving plants generally need about six hours of sunlight to thrive, but sunrise until noon or a midday spell of sunshine is more productive of growth than, say, 3 p.m. until dusk. Is there more light in spring before nearby deciduous trees leaf out? If that is the case, the early spring-blooming bulbs and many native woodlanders can be planted generously. I find it counterproductive and ultimately frustrating to attempt ardent sun-lovers such as pinks or yarrows in dark shade or to inflict the noonday sun on shade-craving primulas.

• Do all the winds of heaven howl through the garden, or is it sheltered by evergreens or buildings? Wind can be buffered with fences or plantings, but an overly close environment in a humid climate can be a breeding ground for fungus. The free flow of air helps keep a garden healthy. However, while delphiniums may not mildew in a breezy garden, they will certainly need stakes. Gardeners aiming for low maintenance on a windy site might forgo delphiniums in favor of self-supporting loosestrife or monkshood.

• What is the earth like — acidic or sweet? Is the soil dense, sticky clay, coarse-textured, dryish sand, decent loam or a mixture of subsoil and rubble left by the construction crew? Of all the specifics of a site, the earth is the most amenable to improvement. There is relatively little one can do about climate, but any soil, no matter how inhospitable to plant growth at the start, responds to consistent generous treatment. (More about that in the next chapter.) An initial careful look at your garden space will make future garden tours more pleasant. No plant will please you for long if it looks as though it would rather be anywhere but in your garden.

With the garden site assessed, the pleasant task of searching out suitable plants begins. "What can I plant," a visitor once asked, "that will come up year after year, flower all summer and take care of itself?" Well, no single plant (that I know of) will do all of that, but a selection of perennials — as few as a dozen different kinds — chosen to succeed one another in bloom, and planted with some thought given to height, habit of growth and color, fills the bill exactly for low maintenance, continuous flowering and relative permanence. In the chapters to come, I will take readers through the flower gardener's year, phase by phase, from the flowers that bloom soon after the snow to those that bide their time until waning summer. Perennials can highlight any corner with bright blossoms and varied leaf shapes, shades and textures, but they reach their full pictorial potential when different kinds are grouped together in a bed or border.

Beds and Borders

A bed is a freestanding island of cultivated ground, usually surrounded by a grassy sea; you walk around a bed viewing it from all sides. A border, in contrast, is backed by a fence, shrubs, hedge, patio or wall and fronted by a path or lawn; you generally view it from one side only. Both arrangements have advantages and disadvantages. A bed of flowers is usually easier to tend and cultivate than a border. Even if a bed is 10 feet across at its widest point, much of the space will come within the gardener's reach from one side or the other, and a few stepping stones bring you even closer to the plants for staking, trimming and bouquet picking. A border, on the other hand, is automatically brought into focus by the wall or by other features of the landscape that define it.

In theory, a bed can be dug anywhere in the landscape, thus allowing a gardener to grow favorite flowers—iris, poppies and pinks, for instance—in a shaded yard's only sunny patch or primroses in the one shadowy corner of an open garden. In practice, however, a flower-decked island in a lawn-sea can look awkward and artificial unless it is thoughtfully positioned, proportioned and shaped in relation to the house or existing trees, evergreens or shrubs— "anchored," as a noted garden designer

puts it. The outline of a bed may be arrow-straight or gracefully curving, depending upon the site and the lay of the land, but busy squiggles or a saw-toothed effect are better avoided.

Because borders are suggested by site parameters such as fences, hedges or driveways, they are easier to site; but they demand certain considerations. If a border's backdrop blocks the sun, plants may grow lanky and weak-kneed. As well, a living background such as shrubs or a hedge can take much of the water and nutrients from nearby perennials, necessitating thorough and more frequent soil enrichment. Finally, given their one-sidedness, densely planted borders can be hard to get at—as I discovered. At Larkwhistle, many of the perennials are planted in 10-foot-wide borders backed by split-rail fencing and inspired by turn-of-the-century gardening books long on romance and short on practicality. Visitors often say (and we silently agree) that these borders are glorious, with plants layered in both time and space, the whole scene changing several times during the season. But tending such a planting becomes a game of wary tiptoeing, a delicate balancing act,

Superb Pink

8

a rather strange yoga routine: hold your breath, make a long stretch, cultivator in hand, to nip budding bindweed under back-of-the-border delphiniums, pivot on the spot and make a grand leap from mid-border to path without squashing coral bells at the edge.

Borders need not be grand and inaccessible to be beautiful. In a newly planted, lattice-enclosed space at Larkwhistle—"the quiet garden," we call it—5-foot-wide borders are a pleasure to tend and ample enough to accommodate three bands of perennials from front to back. Dianthus, mounding hardy geraniums, creeping savory, lady's mantle and lamb's ears tumble over the raised concrete edging. Yard-high bellflowers, obedient plants, Madonna lilies, white bleeding hearts, phlox and veronicas weave through the middle sections, while clumps of delphiniums, *Artemisia lactiflora* and snakeroot spire up in the background. Sweet autumn clematis drapes the lattice with dark green all summer and a flurry of vanilla-scented white stars in September. Even a prickly rugosa rose and a grey-leaved Russian olive tree find space. For the most part, spring bulbs are omitted here, and this as

much as the manageable size of the borders facilitates the work. From mid-June till fall, there are always flowers, never the lavish profusion (and occasional confusion) of the big borders but a pleasant, easygoing show.

While it is possible to squeeze two seasons of bloom into a quite narrow space—a 2½-foot border can grow dwarf spring flowers along the edge and a line of summer perennials behind—longer-blooming, if more complex, pictures are possible on a wider canvas. If a bed or border is from 5 to 10 feet wide, there is room for low plants to spill over the edges and drift back to meet others of medium height, weaving through the middle section, while tall plants congregate toward the back. Perennial gardening evolved as a more naturalistic, less studied alternative to strictly regimented annual bedding—a line of white alyssum, a line of blue lobelia, a line of red geraniums. Although some orderly souls may prefer precise, stepped bands of low, medium and tall perennials, is there any point in copying a summer bedding pattern with permanent plants? Instead, strive for what one old-time writer calls "a rolling contour—plains, foothills and moun-

tains, if one may use so gigantic a simile—the highlands creeping out over the plains and the plains reaching back among the hills."

The Gardener's Art

A newly cleared bed or border, weed-free and raked fine and smooth, is a blank canvas awaiting the gardener's art. The colors of flowers in all their flashing brilliance or subtle shading are what garden artists work with. Plant form, habit and height—whether gracefully arching, low and mounding, tapering skyward or broadly bushy—also figure in the composition.

In designing a bed or border, consider the relative heights of adjacent plants. The 2-foot peach-leaved bellflower looks just fine in front of a yard-high peony but puny against a 7-foot delphinium. A plant's overall form or silhouette also figures in the picture. Broadly rounded or bushy perennials of medium height such as gas plants, false indigo, certain yarrows and artemisias, peonies, hardy geraniums, baby's-breath and daylilies are effective foregrounds for tall, slender hollyhocks, delphiniums, aconites, tiger lilies, snake-roots, *Artemisia lactiflora* and perennial sunflowers.

While this sort of mingling is the essence of perennial gardening, consider, too, that most species show their true colors more effectively if several of the same kind are grouped together. A single coral bell plant is pretty, but so dainty it may go unnoticed, whereas five or six clumps set a foot from one another create a misty breadth of pink or red. A lone *Salvia superba* looks a trifle weedy, but bring five together and the massed purple-violet spikes glow dark and brilliant. One foxglove, lily or iris is lost in the landscape, but a congregation of bell-hung spires, exotic trumpets or multicolored fleurs-de-lis forms an arresting feature. In general, perennials that are slender in habit, and those with dainty flowers in particular, make a more impressive statement when massed. Gertrude Jekyll spoke of setting perennials, again several of one kind, in "drifts" of casually shaped groups—elongated ovals, kidney shapes—rather than three in a triangle, four in a square and so on. Her motives were practical as well as aesthetic. A drift of one kind, she says, "not only has a more pictorial effect, but a thin, long planting does not leave an unsightly empty space when the flowers are done and leaves have perhaps died down."

But not all plants need to be massed. Certain of them are fine as specimens, that is, single plants set in strategic places. Those that qualify as specimens may have opulent, showy blossoms or especially bold and long-lasting leaves, or they may be particularly bulky or wide-spreading so that one plant is a drift all on its own. Some perennials meet all three criteria. A dozen specimen plants, all described in later chapters, include peonies, tall yellow yarrows, hostas, gas plants, baby's-breath, anchusas, loosestrife, cushion euphorbias, Siberian iris, daylilies, false indigo and well-grown clumps of delphiniums, which punctuate the back of a border with violet or sky-blue fountains.

Fill in the Blanks

Although it is entirely possible to design a perennial planting that shows some color from spring until fall, that is not to say that the entire bed or border will be lit up, nonstop, from end to end the whole season through. Lulls in the fireworks are inevitable. Delphiniums, eremurus and globe thistles are routinely cut back when their flowers fade. Empty spots are left where spring bulbs, lovely in their day, have become mere masses of withered leaves. Gaps occur where Oriental poppies go underground for the summer. "Many perennials . . . lose all pride in their appearance as soon as flowering is accomplished," says Louise Beebe Wilder in *Color in My Garden* (1918). "They go to seed most untidily, quite lose their figures and make no effort at all to grow old with dignity and grace."

At Larkwhistle, we solve what Wilder calls the "problem of the bare places" in a few simple but effective ways. I pass them along in the hope that they will help beginners "past the disheartening stages when the blank spaces seem so much more numerous than the full and luxuriant ones."

Perhaps our best way to cover for tulips, daffodils, crown imperials and larger spring bulbs is to plant the bulbs in conjunction with later-rising but ultimately spreading perennials that will hide the fading bulb greenery with a screen of flowers and foliage. If the chosen perennials remain fresh and leafy the season through, so much the better; we have accomplished two crops of flowers in one spot and kept the place pleasantly furnished with foliage.

Thus, at Larkwhistle, most of our peonies and daylilies have attendant groups of daffodils planted close by (but no bulbs within 10 inches of the perennial's crown). As the daffodils bloom, the peonies are just unfurling their spring crimson fans and the daylilies are showing their green spears, but later, the foliage of these perennials will grow up and arch over to form a concealing umbrella. Similarly, tulips, narcissi and Spanish squills weave through groups of phlox, heleniums, yellow yarrows, hardy geraniums, false indigo and the summer daisies—robust perennials all well able to withstand the bulb competition. Pink tulips are particularly nice growing among clumps of succulent gray-leaved *Sedum spectabile*, the showy stonecrops, or half hidden among yarrow's silver, fernlike foliage. Pools of crocuses or blue grape hyacinths lap right up to emerging daylilies or late-rising loosestrife or hostas. Notice that bulbs are teamed with strong-growing summer perennials that can stay put for many years. Other perennials suited to masking bulb defection are meadow rue, ornamental grasses and, for small bulbs only, herbs such as hyssop, rue, southernwood and *Artemisia* 'Lambrook Silver.' Daffodils are especially appealing among delicate, unfurling fern fronds.

Any perennials that are cut back after flowering are best concealed behind a bushy foreground plant with long-lasting leaves. In fact, choosing a selection of plants just for their foliage is another way to mask empty spots. Flower gardeners, by definition, concentrate their efforts on a crop of color, but perennial growers soon learn that many of their permanent plants have rather fleeting flowers—three weeks to a month is the average bloom time. And their leaves may be unappealing, spare or ephemeral. Over the years, I have come to appreciate any plant that maintains a steady show of foliage. Used generously, perennials with fine and lasting leaves go a long way toward keeping a flower garden fresh, full and luxuriant, especially if they are set conspicuously toward the front and midsections of a garden.

Dwarf Iris

11

Perennials for a dry, sunny site

This island bed, which is 25 feet from end to end, could be planted in an exposed part of the lawn or surrounded by a patio. All of the plants marked with an asterisk* are spring-flowering bulbs that grow up through neighboring plants.

1   *Dianthus allwoodii*
2   Bearded iris
3   Three peonies 'Mrs. Livingston Ferrand'
4   Sedum
5* Crocuses
6   *Anthemis tinctoria*
7* Daffodils
8   Bearded iris
9   *Saponaria ocymoides*
10* *Tulipa kaufmanniana* and glory-of-the-snow
11* Darwin tulips
12 *Gypsophila repens*
13* Glory-of-the-snow
14 *Dianthus allwoodii*
15 Bearded iris
16 *Verbascum bombyciferum*
17* Tulips
18 Baby's-breath
19 *Yarrow* 'Moonshine'
20* Crocuses
21 Variegated lemon thyme

22* Daffodils
23 *Papaver orientale*
24* Daffodils
25 *Salvia superba*
26* Siberian scilla
27 Artemisia 'Silver Mound'
28 *Eryngium planum*
29 *Nepeta mussinii*
30* Crocuses
31 *Yucca filamentosa*
32* Daffodils
33 Bearded iris
34 *Dianthus deltoides*
35 Peony 'Kansas Crimson'

36* Snowdrops
37 *Asclepias tuberosa*
38* Lily-flowered tulips
39 *Euphorbia epithymoides*

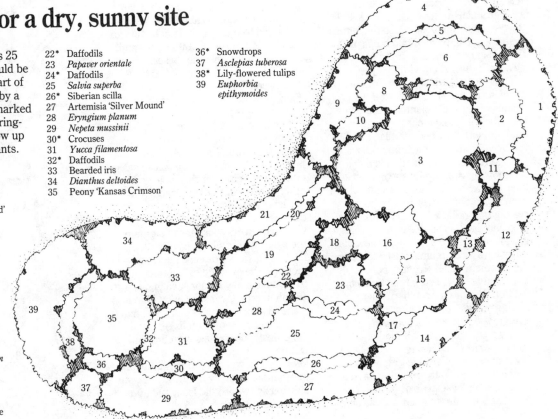

Low-Maintenance Border

This perennial flower border grows at Camp Allsaw, a children's summer camp that is attended only during the summer months. It needs to be brightly colored, easy to care for and, as the camp teaches orgainc gardening methods, relatively pest-free. It is 40 feet long by 10 feet wide.

1 Hosta (Cultivar A)
2 Bleeding heart 'Luxuriant'
3 Lily
4 Daylily (Cultivar A)
5 *Gypsophila repens*
6 *Aconitum napellus* 'Bicolor'
7 *Helenium autumnale*
8 Daylily (Cultivar B)
9 Coral bells
10 Yarrow 'Moonshine'
11 Rugosa rose 'Jens Munk'
12 *Monarda didyma*
13 Bellflower 'Blue Clips'
14 Salvia 'East Friesland'
15 Lily (white)
16 Purple loosestrife
17 *Artemisia lactiflora*
18 Rugosa rose 'Jens Munk'
19 Shasta daisy, double
20 Yarrow 'Gold Plate'
21 Phlox (white)
22 Perennial sunflower
23 Tradescantia
24 Bergamot (pink)
25 *Heuchera sanguinea*
26 *Sedum spectabile*
27 Purple loosestrife
28 *Aconitum napellus*
29 Daylily 'Hyperion'
30 Lily
31 Hosta (Cultivar B)
32 Daylily (Cultivar C)
33 *Heuchera sanguinea*

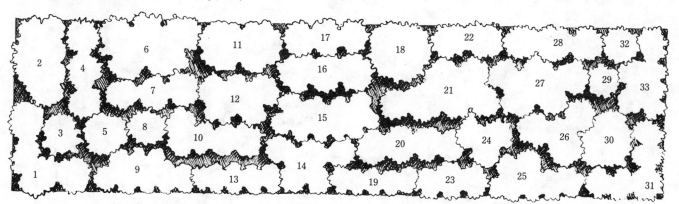

13

Section of a Larkwhistle Border

This border section is 30 feet long and 10 feet wide, making it spectacular but difficult to tend when a certain amount of stepping in the border becomes necessary. The color theme here is blue and pink, with touches of red and white and, later in the season, a shift into yellows. The plants marked with an asterisk* are spring-flowering bulbs that grow up through the neighboring plants.

1   Double arabis
2* Crocuses
3   *Nepeta mussinii*
4   *Dianthus arenarius*
5   Daylily 'Hyperion' and narcissus
6   Lily
7   Baby's-breath
8   Peony 'Sea Shell'
9* Small spring bulbs
10 Lily 'Wanda'
11 *Pyrethrum roseum*
12 Candytuft
13 *Phlox paniculata* and narcissus
14 *Fritillaria imperialis*
15 *Eryngium alpinum*
16 *Sedum spectabile*
17* Tulips (pink)
18 *Phlox subulata* (lavender)
19 Flowering crab
20* Narcissus
21 Lavender 'Hidcote Blue'
22 Clematis 'Pink Chiffon'
23 *Aconitum napellus* 'Bicolor'
24 Yarrow 'Moonshine'
25* Narcissus
26 Delphinium 'Summer Skies'
27 *Helenium autumnale*
28 Lily
29* Crocuses
30 *Stachys lanata*
31 Hollyhocks, single pink
32 Baby's-breath
33* Narcissus
34 *Papaver orientale*
35 *Heuchera sanguinea* (pink)
36 Siberian iris 'Orville Fay'
37 Peony 'Crinkled White'
38* *Scilla campanulata*
39* Tulips (white)
40 *Dianthus caesius*
41 *Phlox subulata* (pink)

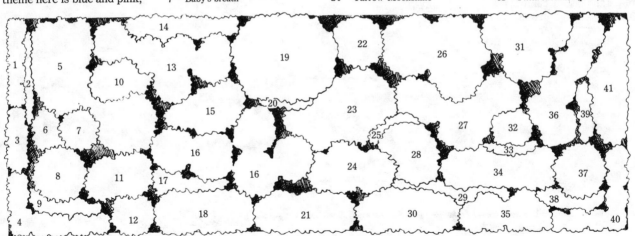

Earthly Basics

Fundamentals for perennials

CHAPTER 2

L abor is the house that love dwells in," says a Russian proverb. Like any loving link, that between gardener and garden requires care and maintenance. First, land must be cleared and plants sown or set in place. Thereafter, every garden, even one stocked with only the most self-sufficient perennials, needs routine attention: weeding, watering and, as a foundation for all, the creation and sustenance of good soil.

Whether a flower garden takes shape

15

from a detailed paper plan or evolves in a more spontaneous fashion, its beauty ultimately depends on plants that are robust, healthy and obviously thriving, plants that have been chosen to suit the garden site and then are set in good-hearted ground. It has been said that any soil that grows a decent crop of potatoes or cabbages will grow perennials well. This does not minimize the fertility that perennials need but rather emphasizes that most are hungry, husky plants that, in order to reach their full potential, must sink their roots into the same sort of nourishing earth that produces bushels of edible roots and greens. The fact that perennials stay in one place for years is a further inducement to provide them with fertility from the start.

But even before that, sod breaking might be in order, unless a gardener decides to cultivate perennials in an established vegetable garden—not a bad idea, considering that the land there is already cleared and probably well enriched. Clearing land by hand is a gardener's most difficult task, but it is also work that, if done thoroughly, need be done only once. By contrast, extracting quack grass and choking bindweed

from the crowns of one's precious perennials is an ongoing and (probably) a losing battle; every scrap of root left in a perennial bed will come back.

"Skim off the turf," one gardening book blithely instructs as the first step toward making a garden—as if turf were akin to cream floating on milk. At Larkwhistle, on the other hand, the recipe for converting a strip of lawn or a corner of a field into a new flower bed goes something more like this:

First, we delineate the space by marking off straight-edged borders with stakes and string or curving outlines with a length of garden hose wiggled about until it describes the desired graceful sweep. Then, we slice along the defined edge with a sharp, flat-edged spade and slice the enclosed turf into a grid of chunks somewhat smaller than a foot square. These will have to be lifted, so they should be kept as small as can be easily managed. Using a spading fork, we pry loose a chunk of sod, flip it earth-side up and whack away at the roots with the fork tines to loosen as much of the precious topsoil as possible. Then we spear the chunk of sod, lift it and shake out the topsoil; sandy soil falls away more readily than

sticky clay. On clay soil, try to time sod breaking so that the ground is at its most crumbly, not sodden in early spring or baked to an unyielding crust in the heat of summer.

Gradually—an hour a day of sod skimming is a workout—the area is completely cleared. Good quality sods may be used to create a new lawn area—water them as soon as they are positioned—or the sods can be piled by themselves upside down in an out-of-the-way place to compost. A tarpaulin over the pile discourages the grass from sprouting. Twitch-grass roots or perennial weeds soon infest a regular compost pile. When the space is stripped of sod, we rake the earth to catch stray roots, rocks and rubbish. If the area can be left fallow for several weeks, any elusive roots will sprout, and a bit of spot digging should catch the last of the troublemakers.

Clearing land is the surest way to acquaint oneself with the tilth and texture of a garden's soil, which may range from pure sand (coarse-textured, open, warm and dry) to pure clay (fine-textured, cool, gummy when wet, brick-hard when dry and fit only for ceramics). Thankfully, most gardeners be-

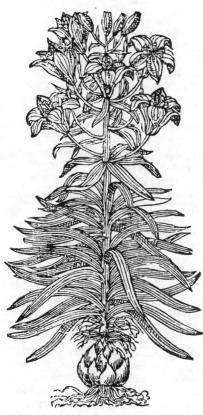

Fiery Red Lily

gin with something in between, with any luck, loam—a balanced, evenly textured blend of sand, clay and organic material. When we dug into the hayfield that has since become our garden, what we found was pale sandy loam, so dust-dry in August that it flowed through our fingers like sand in an hourglass. Twelve years of organic enrichment now show in darker color, better moisture retention and increasingly robust plant growth.

Over time, organic enrichment of the earth is accomplished by adding spongy, partly decayed material such as animal manure, straw, leaves or other plant remains that will replenish and boost its humus content. There was a time when, in the interests of soil improvement, my partner and I climbed the fence of an abandoned zoo and hauled burlap sacks of water buffalo and yak manure home on the streetcar to a cindery city garden; but today, our sources of organic matter are more conventional. Farmyard manure forms the foundation of our perennial beds. We look for manure that has stood in a neighboring barnyard long enough to turn earth-dark and crumbly. Less fertile than fresher stuff, well-aged manure

nevertheless mixes more easily with the soil and can be used generously without fear of overstimulating growth or burning plant roots, as the fresh manure might do. Fallen leaves, too, provide us with humus. According to tests at the University of Connecticut, newly fallen leaves exude chemicals that actually inhibit plant growth, but leaves left in a heap for a season or two break down into a finely textured fertilizer called leaf mold, which can be spread as mulch or turned into the earth for primroses, lilies, Siberian iris and others that appreciate spongy ground.

Another source of organic matter is compost, the heart of any good garden and a reminder that nature efficiently reuses everything to foster new growth. Recipes abound for making perfect compost in a few weeks, usually by shredding ingredients, layering them with a certain ratio of fresh manure, turning the steaming heap and keeping moisture levels just so. The end result is a near-perfect plant food, crumbly, dark and moist, "like the richest chocolate cake," in the words of Vita Sackville-West.

Some gardeners, however, must rely on store-bought organic matter. Peat

17

moss contains almost no plant food but helps to bind sandy soils and loosen clay. Although it holds 20 times its weight in water, the moss should be dampened before it is used and then mixed thoroughly with the soil; dry lumps act as wicks to steal water from the surrounding ground. Damp peat moss mixed with an equal volume of bagged, composted manure is also convenient organic matter for gardeners without access to farmyard manure. Add a spadeful each of bone meal (or rock phosphate) and wood ashes to a wheelbarrow of blended peat moss and manure, and you have a nourishing, humusy mix that will improve the texture and fertility of any soil.

To prepare new flower beds at Larkwhistle, we spread a generous layer – 6 inches is not too much – of organic matter over a bed, whiten the surface with bone meal and spade the works deeply into the topsoil. Rototilling would also do the job. For deeply rooted, long-lived perennials, we prepare special planting holes, 18 inches across and 16 inches deep, by piling topsoil to one side, digging out and hauling away subsoil and backfilling with humus and topsoil well stirred together. Plants that appreciate

such a spot include aconites, baptisias, the tall campanulas, daylilies, delphiniums, gas plants, heleniums, Siberian iris, snakeroot, lilies, loosestrife, peonies, tall summer phlox and Japanese anemones. Where three or more of these perennials are grouped together, consider excavating an oval 5 feet by 2 feet rather than a series of holes. Enriched to a foot deep or more, such a space will accommodate three of the husky perennials just mentioned, with the individual plants spaced 18 inches apart.

Many perennials benefit from top dressing. If we have a goodly supply of very old, crumbly manure or fine compost, we often spread a layer around the crowns of the hungriest perennials. This ideally is done in spring, but any time is better than never. Plants that are treated in this way benefit from a shot of liquid plant food every time it rains, and earthworms eventually do the work of taking the surface organic matter into the soil.

Where topsoil is thin and starved or where unyielding subsoil ("hard-pan") or bedrock lie just beneath the soil surface, raised beds are useful. Beds can be defined with low stone walls, chunky

rocks, railroad ties one or two high or with 2-by-8-inch cedar boards secured with 2-by-4-inch rot-resistant stakes pounded into the ground on the outside of the boards. Fill such beds with imported topsoil mixed with organic matter, or if patience allows, use the spaces as composting or leaf storage areas for a season or two, after which the finished compost or leaf mold can be turned into whatever earth is there and the works topped up with extra soil, if necessary.

Perennial Care

"It is one thing to make a perennial border and quite another to maintain it," says Richardson Wright. Granted, but if a garden is conscientiously cleared and generously fertilized at the start, the necessary after-care is accomplished with far greater ease. This garden maintenance includes roughly five tasks. Weeding and cultivating I count as one, because they usually happen together. Another three are watering, staking and trimming, this last job subdivided into pruning, removing dead flower heads and cutting back perennials in fall. The remaining chore involves taking steps to keep plants relatively unmolested by insects and diseases.

As for the last task, the story of disease in our flower garden is, thankfully, short. In more than a decade of growing a wide variety of food and flowering plants, we have used no chemical fertilizers, herbicides or pesticides at Larkwhistle. A flourishing, healthy, abundant garden speaks volumes, I think, about the efficacy of generous and consistent organic treatment. Occasionally, a few peony stems drop from a botrytis infection, or the odd iris rhizome falls victim to bacterial soft rot; the phlox may mildew or hollyhock leaves sprout ugly orange spots. These few afflictions are fungal in nature, and while most are seasonal, none are terminal.

The old adage about "an ounce of prevention" is appropriate in the garden. Sanitation is our first line of defence. Diseased plant parts are pruned away and either buried in the center of an active (hot) compost heap, thrown away or burned. Treating the soil kindly, too, is a preventive measure; tests have shown that plants growing in humus-rich earth are less susceptible to mil-

dew. And fungal diseases are less apt to afflict perennials that are given adequate elbowroom or are growing in breezy gardens. Wise is the gardener who does not routinely spray a shower of water on the flower beds of an evening; fungus thrives where leaves are damp all night. Working in a wet or dewy garden can also abet the spread of disease.

The tale of insect pests is even shorter. For the most part, bugs are blasé about perennials; vegetables are more to their taste. In 12 years, we have yet to encounter an appreciable pest problem in the flower garden, and we have used nothing more potent than insecticidal soap to rid roses or honeysuckle of aphids or to clear out nests of earwigs. ("At least they die clean," quipped one visitor.) In damp weather, slugs munch their way through a shady salad bar of primroses and hostas. A foray into the garden after dark with a flashlight, however, brings the night crawlers to light for slippery hand-picking, an approach we also use by day to catch leaf-rolling worms and other obvious insects.

"Nature's censors," insects have been called. It is a maxim of organic culture

White Cinquefoil

19

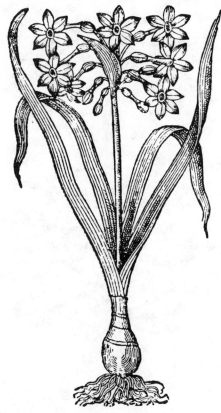

French Daffodil

that well-fed, strong-growing, lively plants are less attractive to bugs than any that are weak, ailing or otherwise struggling. (Could this explain why recent transplants are often chewed?) Again, selecting perennials that are suitable to your site and setting them in nourishing earth are important preventive measures. Also, a garden that grows a diversity of plants is less apt to be bothered by bugs. Grow only irises, and every iris borer around will find the place that provides their favorite food and lots of it.

Not all insects are anathema to a good garden. Ladybugs and praying mantids gobble aphids. Parasitic wasps prey on bugs that prey on plants. A gardener who hauls out the big guns to spray harsh, nonselective chemicals kills friend and foe alike and risks injuring bug-eating birds. The garden's delicate balance is knocked off kilter, and the next season may bring more bothersome pests rather than fewer. Better to aim for balance and encourage birds with suitable shrubs and enticing birdhouses. Toads and snakes, too, are useful garden residents. Larkwhistle is home to snakes of several stripes. A slender sea-green one lives in a dry-built stone wall; a graceful garter snake slides out from under a concealing umbrella of hosta leaves and—after a meal of slugs, one hopes—stretches over the rim of the lily pool for a drink. Tolerance, of course, has limits. Twice, after recovering from the shock, we have had to shoo away massasauga rattlesnakes, fierce-looking but timid creatures that are more than welcome to eat all the bugs and mice they like—outside the garden.

Weeds are also unwelcome in a flower garden. Variously defined as "flowers out of place" by Wordsworth and "poor creatures whose virtues have not yet been discovered" by Emerson, they mar its beauty, steal food and water from ornamentals and often host harmful insects. Like the garden's rightful dwellers, weeds are perennial, biennial or annual. Perennial weeds, as noted earlier, had better be rooted out entirely before you set in a single garden plant, or they will trouble you ever after. Annuals and biennials should be grabbed before they run to seed because, in the words of an old saw, "one year's seeding, seven years' weeding."

There is really no shortcut here. Weeding is a hands-and-knees or a stooping job, but if it is not left until the emergency stage, it can be as relaxing and gratifying as any garden task. One garden writer tells of studying her French verbs as she worked her way along a flower bed, the textbook open on the grass beside the weed basket. I like to listen to music or play the radio. In any case, unless weeding is done thoroughly – that means extracting interlopers root and all – it will have to be done again. "Cutting the tops off weeds," writes Louise B. Wilder, "has the same effect as cutting children's hair; it thickens the growth." Turn weeds into the earth, and they will probably rise again.

Every gardener, no doubt, has favorite weeding tools. A curving grapefruit knife is useful for turning out plantain or other bothersome greenery from mats of creeping thyme and the like. Fingers work just fine on most weeds rooted in Larkwhistle's sandy soil, but a sturdy forked metal weeder comes in handy in clay gardens or wherever stubborn burdock – whose taproot "goes deeper than conscience," as I once read – or curled dock or bladder campion refuse to budge.

Where borders flank a lawn, encroaching grass is often a problem. If the border is edged with rocks, unchecked roots soon insinuate themselves under the rocks and become next to impossible to weed out. I once saw a gardener pouring gasoline along a stone-edged flower bed in a desperate (and futile) attempt to kill the grass. What he ended up with was a hideous, oily edge and more grass moving away from the gas and into the flowers. Much better, I think, to keep grass at least 8 inches from front-of-the-border plants or edging rocks at the start, and then, twice a year, to cut a scant 1-inch swath along the grassy verge with a sharp, flat-bladed spade – I am no fan of the flimsy rocking-horse tools sold as edgers – to remove the narrow band of sod along with attached grass runners that are invading the garden beds.

More Maintenance

When watering becomes necessary, it is best done deeply. Surface wetting does more harm than good by encouraging plant roots to remain shallow and thus susceptible to drought. Since we carry water by hand to our garden, we have found ways both to minimize the garden's need for water and to maximize the benefits when we do water. In areas where water consumption is restricted over summer, such methods are also appropriate.

•Add large amounts of spongy organic matter to the soil before planting perennials, and enrich deeply to encourage the growth of deep-rooted, long-lived plants.

•Early in the season, mulch thirsty perennials with compost, decayed leaves, straw or what have you. Tall, late-blooming thirsty plants, such as phlox, aconite, helenium, lythrum and heliopsis, benefit most from mulch, as do any plants that prefer damp ground, such as Siberian iris.

•Cultivate soon after a rain or an artificial watering to retain moisture.

•In a dry garden or drought-prone area, let the bulk of your perennials be drought-resistant. These include yarrows, mulleins, pinks, arabis, iberis, creeping phlox, most alliums, *Salvia superba*, bearded iris, lamb's ears and others mentioned as such in the forthcoming chapters.

•Sculpt the earth around plants so that water stays where it should. If I am hauling buckets of water to phlox, I do not want half of it running into the path or trickling around neighboring plants.

•Add fish emulsion (or equivalent) to the water occasionally, or brew some manure tea, especially if plants are pining.

•Give watering priority to wilting plants or any that are on the verge of flowering in mid-drought.

•Learn a rain dance.

Like weeding, staking is better done before the need for it becomes critical. A budded peony is much simpler to support than one that has already sprawled. Besides top-heavy peonies, perennials that routinely need staking at Larkwhistle include tall bearded iris, delphiniums, balloon flowers, baby's-breath, the taller hardy asters, anchusas, perennial sunflowers and tall trumpet lilies growing in breezy places.

Use slim green canes and twist-ties for iris and lilies, stout 1-by-2-inch lumber wound with strong string for delphiniums, and for others, follow the staking methods described in the discussion of individual perennials in the following chapters.

Once a week, during the summer, we do a "dead-heading" tour of the flower beds. All that is needed is a pair of pruning shears to snip away spent blooms or seedpods and a bucket or bushel basket for compostable refuse. Dead-heading not only enhances the garden picture by focusing attention on plants in bloom, it also prevents some prolific seeders from joining the ranks of a gardener's self-inflicted weeds. Dead-heading may also encourage further flowering.

Garden work is seasonal, with spring the busiest time followed by a fairly relaxed spell, once staking is done and before the fall flurry of activity. Whatever the season, garden chores are no hardship for me. The April days spent trimming and sprucing the flower beds, the June mornings given to shearing back early-flowering edging plants or staking peonies laden with promising buds, the late-summer evenings occupied in hauling buckets of reviving water (perhaps laced with fish emulsion) to thirsty phlox or heleniums are pleasant, relaxed times that provide opportunities to observe the garden's progress and to enjoy the flowers close up in an active, cooperative way.

On the subject of garden work, Richard Eichenauer, a master gardener who lives in British Columbia, says, "It's no bother at all. It's what I live for."

I echo the sentiment.

Early Spring

Small bulbs to follow the snow

Crocus

CHAPTER 3

For me, the smell of spring air—"essence of fertility," one old-time garden writer calls it—has always been the season's most delicious sign. Breathing is deeper in spring. Our faces turned toward the sun, winter coats and boots having slipped away like a reptile's useless skin, we are forever filling our lungs and exhaling a satisfied, "Ah, spring." Even as a child growing up on a city street, all concrete and ceaseless traffic, I sensed this invisible signal with pleasure. Now that I tend a coun-

23

try garden, I welcome spring more than ever, for while my nose sniffs out the best scent of the year, my eyes quest for color.

One week the garden is snowbound and bleak; the next, if south winds and sunshine persist, there are flowers. Sparks of color appear along the receding edge of the snow or glow promisingly just under the last fragile crusts of ice. Snowdrops (*Galanthus* spp) and winter aconites (*Eranthis* spp) are traditionally—but not invariably, in our garden—the earliest spring flowers. Under the snow, they have been silently active; spring thaw often finds these patient bulbs budded and ready, waiting for the first warm nudge.

Snowdrops
(*Galanthus* spp)

Bloom: early spring
Height: 2-3 inches
Color: white
Needs: afternoon shade

Snowdrops are not the fragile creatures they seem to be; indeed, part of their appeal lies in the contrast between their delicate appearance and their sturdy reality. Nature has fashioned these early flowers to push through crusty snow and hard ground and to cope with cold.

Considering what the season throws at them in the way of snowstorms, sleet, driving rain, splashing mud and hard frosts, snowdrops last a long time in fine form.

Early planting is essential, as soon as bulbs are available and certainly no later than mid-September. Snowdrops resent well-intentioned meddling—being dug up and moved around and, especially, being kept out of the ground any length of time. But left alone, they will increase by offsets and (if you're lucky) seeds for decades.

Crocuses
(*Crocus* spp)

Bloom: early spring
Height: 2-6 inches
Color: orange, lavender, blue, white, yellow, cream
Needs: full sun

In a sunnier part of the garden, the first patches of color are likely to be buds of wee *Crocus ancyrensis* poking through their tight bundles of spiky leaves. In our garden, this 2-inch Turkish wildflower usually outpaces even impatient snowdrops or winter aconites. Several dozen corms, 50 or so, are best, since they are inexpensive, take up next to no room and spread quickly to make a splash of warm color in a cool spring garden.

This first crocus is followed in short order by a clutch of its wild kin. In some catalogues, they are dubbed "snowcrocus" because of their precipitous flowering, but by any name, they are among spring's best gifts to gardeners. A favorite of mine is *Crocus sieberi*, with its small cupped blossoms of cool lilac blue warmed by an orange center and scarlet stigmata.

From the variable species, *Crocus chrysanthus*, a host of hardy, early snowcrocuses have descended, among them 'Snow Bunting,' 'Blue Bird,' 'Cream Beauty' and 'Zwanenburg Bronze.' These are the most generous of spring plants, increasing rapidly to form flowery mounds of clear color—blue, white, yellow, cream—along border edges, down rock garden slopes or in any sunny corner where they need not be disturbed for years. All rush into

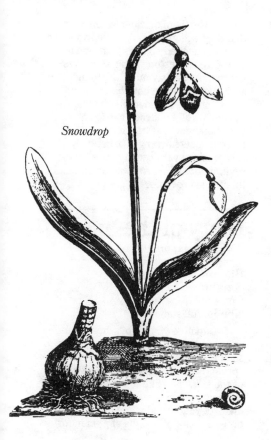

Snowdrop

bloom at the first hint of warmth. For best effect, these small corms should be planted in informal groups of, say, 25 to 50 at the front of a flowerbed. If later-flowering dwarf perennials are set between the groups, color will carry on into summer.

Many gardeners miss the early wild crocuses and count on the fat Dutch hybrids for first color. While I would not forgo the species already described, I cannot imagine the spring garden without lots of these late crocuses—drifts of purple and gold, white and lavender, weaving through sprouting perennials along border edges, clustered around crimson peony shoots and emerging daylilies or skirting the sunny side of shrubs. The crocus is an informal flower; it never looks its best dotted along a single straight line (few flowers do). Rather, I like to plant crocuses in winding bands, three to five corms deep, trailing off to a few scattered flowers at the edge of a group. A mixed lot—all crocus colors are harmonious—creates a cheerful spring tapestry.

Remember to associate the corms with perennials that can stay in place for many years; the crocuses themselves will not need digging and dividing until they show by fewer and smaller flowers that they are overcrowded.

I have found that crocuses of all kinds, wild or tame, take care of themselves, provided their few requirements are met. First, they crave sun for most of the day. Second, if protected from cold north winds, they flower earlier and longer. Finally, experts agree that the soil for crocuses should be nourishing and fairly light. Heavy clay, shade, soggy spots and soil clogged with fresh manure all lead to failure.

Crocuses are planted about 4 inches deep, from August through October. This slightly deeper planting may help to discourage chipmunks and squirrels from snacking on the corms. In subsequent seasons, a top dressing of crumbly compost or very old (or bagged) manure keeps them fit, but even if you miss this step, the crocus corms should take care of themselves. However strong the tidying urge, it is important after crocuses have blossomed to let the grasslike foliage ripen thoroughly to nourish next spring's crop of flowers; when it is withered and yellow, the foliage pulls away with a gentle tug, leaving corms in place.

Winter Aconite
(Eranthis spp)

Bloom: early spring
Height: 2-3 inches
Color: yellow
Needs: afternoon shade

Picture a buttercup sitting on a frilly green ruff of leaves atop a 2- or 3-inch stem, and you have a fair view of the winter aconite. Snow melts to reveal round buds and arching stems already unfolding. In no time, there are flowers. Never mind that they will be hit with another round of winter. The flowers simply close and bide their time.

Winter aconites grow from small, brown, oddly shaped tuberous roots. Bulb suppliers usually have eranthis on hand in August. It is essential that gardeners order them early and tuck the tubers in the ground the day they arrive. Plant them 3 inches deep and the same distance apart. Since winter aconites grow best in precisely the same soil and sites that suit snowdrops and since the two bloom in sync, an early garden picture consists of a nice mingling of white and gold.

Early Iris
(Iris spp)

Bloom: early spring
Height: 12-24 inches
Color: blue
Needs: full sun

Gardeners have always been enthusiastic about any flower decked in azure. Fortunately, compared with other seasons, spring is generous with blossoms of this color—bluebells, grape hyacinths, glory-of-the-snow and violets. A less familiar source of spring blue is an early little iris, *Iris reticulata*; the last name refers to the netted or "reticulated" coat that covers the oval bulbs.

Reticulata iris look exotic and challenging, but they are, in fact, easy to grow. They need lots of sun, all day if possible. Soil of preference is a light sandy loam, well drained and sweet (no wonder they have taken to our garden). Heavier ground should be treated with a dressing of coarse sand, small stone chips, decayed maple leaves or old manure—but not peat moss; earth tending to acidity needs crushed limestone. The right setting for these gems not only shows them off but also ensures that they will grow well. I like to see the early iris nestled on the south side of good-sized limestone rocks that have been sunk partway into the ground; such rocks provide both background and safety from cold spring winds. Although a well-built rock garden is an ideal home for many spring bulbs, even three boulders arranged artistically in a corner of the yard can give shelter to several dozen *Iris reticulata* and a handful of wild crocuses.

Glory-of-the-Snow
(Chionodoxa spp)

Bloom: early spring
Height: 4-6 inches
Color: blue
Needs: full sun

In a small town nearby, there is an expanse of front lawn that becomes a solid blue carpet for a few weeks each spring. I am exceedingly fond of glory-of-the-snow and like to see them streaming along a sunny border among drifts of yellow and white crocuses, congregating under boughs of golden forsythia or exotic magnolias or lighting up a rock garden. Chionodoxas are determined self-sowers, but they are also so unobtrusive—at first they look just like seedling onions—that I let them stay where they settle. Their spring show is brilliant but brief, and the narrow leaves die back quickly, leaving no sign that the small bulbs are hidden underground.

Chionodoxas will take to almost any soil that is not brick-hard or waterlogged. They prefer sunshine for a good part of the day and earth that is porous with organic matter or gritty with sand or small stones. The bulbs are planted in the fall, about 3 inches deep and a few inches apart. After that, the work is done.

Scilla
(*Scilla* spp)

Bloom: early spring
Height: 4-6 inches
Color: blue, white
Needs: shade

Like chionodoxas, scillas are small, early, self-reliant and serenely blue pe-

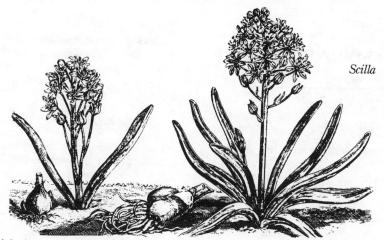

Scilla

rennials that grow from bulbs. They flourish, however, in the shade. There is no trick to establishing a small colony or even an extravagant mass of the familiar bluebells. Plant them in the fall, 3 or 4 inches deep and a few inches apart, in organically enriched ground (as for snowdrops), and then leave them alone ever after to increase at will.

Big bear of the scillas is *Scilla campanulata*, the Spanish bluebell, last of all to bloom and an important element in our May garden pictures in the perennial beds. Bulbs of this species are large (several inches across), white and

fleshy; the long, smooth leaves lie close to the ground. Sturdy flower stalks grow all of 18 inches tall, their upper halves decorated with many pure blue flaring bells. This is a showy plant for flower beds in light shade or sun, provided that the soil remains evenly moist. Spanish squills combine beautifully with cream or yellow intermediate iris or tall late tulips of any color; the white-flowered variety gleams among ferns, primroses or trilliums. Plant bulbs of *S. campanulata* 4 to 6 inches deep—the larger the bulb, the greater the depth—in well-drained loam.

27

Grape Hyacinth

(Muscari spp)

Bloom: early spring
Height: 4-6 inches
Color: blue, white
Needs: partial to full sun

Earlier blue is supplied by several species of grape hyacinth, or muscari. The common name alludes to the arrangement of the small, rounded flowers in tapered clusters, like bunches of grapes, atop 4-to-6-inch stems. Even the rankest novice will succeed with grape hyacinths. The accommodating bulbs thrive in almost any soil short of swampland, take to any reasonably sunny site and return with vigor after even the harshest winter. In several seasons, they increase to form satisfying pools of blue among the white and yellow daffodils, blue ribbons binding shrub borders where polyanthus primroses grow or small fountains of azure between the crimson peony shoots just unfurling.

A word about situating grape hyacinths in a border: because their foliage is uninteresting and their lingering seedpods downright ugly, muscari bulbs are best planted where they will be hidden by perennials that leaf out after the blue show is over. Peonies are perfect for the task, as are daylilies, phlox, yarrows, hardy geraniums or Siberian iris. Remember, too, that (unlike other bulbs) all species of grape hyacinth send up leaves in the fall. This is a handy trait; the foliage indicates the bulbs' location so that one is not tempted to tuck a few crocus corms in that "empty" space.

Spring Standbys

Wild daffodils, primroses and their hardy allies

Jonquil

CHAPTER 4

Spring is a gentle season. Against the dark earth and a backdrop of fresh green, the early garden is a harmony of yellow, white and orange flowers complemented by lavender and blue petals that match the sky in brilliance.

Primrose
(*Primula* spp)

Bloom: May-June
Height: 2 inches to 2 feet
Color: every color
Needs: partial shade

All the colors of this spring spectrum are represented by just one plant group, the primroses, among the most generous of the early comers but so quiet and dependable that they are perfectly in tune with the unfolding season.

No spring perennials bloom as long—a full five weeks on average—and no perennials at all, with the exception of bearded irises, display as wide and lovely a color range as primroses. A late April walk along our little, ambling primrose path—a curving, yard-wide border skirting the shady side of budding lilacs—takes us past flowers that are pink, mauve and wine-purple, butter-yellow and cream, Indian-red, toffee-brown, golden tan and all shades of blue from light to navy.

Primroses are more than willing to add their fresh, simple flowers to the spring scene, provided their two needs, shade and moisture, are met. This may translate into a north- or east-facing border against a house or fence, the cool side of shrubs or a bed of humusy loam under the flickering shade of birch trees. Any gardener blessed with a damp, wooded corner by a stream or pond is set to grow primroses supremely well.

The lowly primrose has a big appetite for organic matter. After stripping away the turf from our prospective primrose path, we set about turning in an 8-inch layer of crumbly, dark cow manure mixed with dampened peat moss. That done and the border raked fine and smooth, we tuck in seedling primroses about 10 inches apart—three to five yellows overlapping an equal drift of white or reddish brown. A manure mulch laid down the next spring and the next helps to maintain fertility and conserve moisture. With such encouragement, stripling primroses soon wax into robust clumps, sending up perfect fountains of multihued flowers.

But sooner or later, even the most pampered primroses begin to show a weakened ring of leaves around an increasingly bald and woody center. It will be time then, sometime in June after the current crop of bloom is over, to renew a patch. After prying the shallow-rooted primroses out of the ground with a sturdy trowel or hand fork, ease a clump apart by hand—the dividing lines are easy to see—into one- or two-crowned divisions. Retaining only the liveliest outer growth, reset the plantlets in freshly enriched earth. If organic matter is in short supply, consider spot-enriching—several trowelsful of humus under each primrose—rather than applying a thin dressing over all. Water with dilute fish emulsion or manure tea, a brew made of manure dissolved in plenty of water, and see that the plants do not lack for moisture over the summer.

The least fussy of primulas, cowslips (*Primula veris*) do well enough with a modicum of shade and moisture but respond to better conditions with exuberant and extended spring bloom.

Where the environment suits them, cowslips naturalize freely. Under the trees that line a local farm driveway, scores of them, self-sown like any native wildflower, light up the shade.

More demanding of moisture, oxlips (*Primula elatior*) carry clustered soft yellow flowers that are larger and flatter than cowslips. But of all the wild primulas, the sentimental favorite of old-world gardeners is the common or English primrose (*P. vulgaris*), whose typical tuft of wrinkled oval leaves all but disappears under a swarm of flowers of simple primrose yellow, the color of fresh butter, one to a stem.

Crosses between primula species have given rise to a sturdy race of garden primroses, the polyanthus of countless colors and many variations in form. One seed-raised novelty, a hands-down favorite with garden visitors, is the gold-laced polyanthus. A sharp, light yellow edging laid over a blackish background gives this flower's 5 petals the appearance of 10. Then there are the double primroses, like small true roses of pink, peach or lavender.

As cowslips, oxlips, English primroses and polyanthus complete their blooming season, the star primrose of Japan (*Primula sieboldii*) begins to open elegant flowers—white, shell-pink, mauve or deep rose—as lacy as snowflakes. Rather than forming crowded clumps, this easiest, hardiest and most beautiful of primroses has the unusual attribute (for a primula) of a creeping rootstock that travels just underground

and re-emerges as a new tuft of softly crumpled foliage a little way from the mother plant. This primula retreats underground entirely during the hot summer months, only to show its lovely leaves and blossoms again next May. Our star primroses thrive in sun—since sun is all we have to give them—but according to all accounts, they would appreciate a half-day's shade in warmer gardens.

Two more oriental beauties complete our list. *Primula denticulata* is among the loveliest of spring perennials. Atop 10-inch stems, many small white, lavender or purple-red flowers, each petal notched or toothed as the Latin species name suggests, are arranged in perfect balls of bloom. It flowers very early, so we keep flowerpots on hand to pop over our *denticulatas* to ward off frosts that would spoil the bloom.

Primula japonica, a tall late-flowering species belonging to the "candelabra" group, hoists strong, 2½-foot stems bearing intense magenta-crimson flowers in ascending tiers above lush rosettes of lettuce-green leaves. A true bog primula, *japonica* is at home on the banks of a stream but can be made comfortable in well-manured loam that

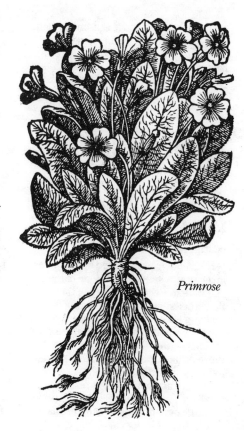

Primrose

31

is kept nicely moist the season through. Our dozen clumps, again raised from seed, share space with hostas, Jacob's ladder and spiderwort in an 18-inch-deep raised bed filled with topsoil, manure and peat moss. All of them seem to enjoy a drink of cooled dishwater.

Species Daffodils

(*Narcissus* spp)

Bloom: April, May
Height: 3-12 inches
Color: yellow, white
Needs: partial shade to partial sun, neutral soil

If I could grow only two spring perennials, primroses would be one of them and daffodils the other. When the flowerbeds are alight with daffodils swaying above simple blue-green leaves, I am almost ready to agree with an early writer that "the high point of the year has been reached, that all that follows is anticlimax."

The genus *Narcissus* is a relatively small one containing perhaps 40 species all told; some botanists recognize as few as 12, since it is not clear where wild

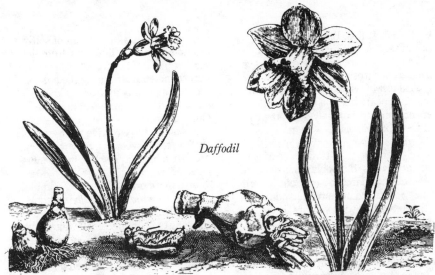

Daffodil

narcissi leave off and cultivated sorts begin. These wildflowers, the so-called "species daffodils," are the parents of all of our cultivated daffodils, of which there are thousands.

Standing all of 3 inches tall, with flowers no larger than a dime, *N. minimus*, the smallest and earliest to bloom of all daffodils, is a perfect replica in miniature of the tall yellow trumpet types. For years now, it has grown freely in our chilly garden, where it stages a brave small show in mid-April.

The soil recommended for the little bulbs is gritty and neutral (a pH of around 6 or 7), not clogged with manure or overly sweetened with lime. Our colony grows in unimproved sandy loam with a surface mulch of stone chips; for company, there are the silver rosettes of encrusted saxifrages and other scaled-down alpine plants.

Close to *Narcissus minimus* grows another Spaniard, *N. triandrus albus*, poetically called angel's tears. The name is apt. Its tiny ivory cups turn gracefully

32

Essential Reading

Special Offer to Harrowsmith Readers

If this handbook has sparked your interest in perennial gardening, you will want Patrick Lima's highly acclaimed new full-color book, *The Harrowsmith Perennial Garden,* a large-format guide to planning, planting and maintaining perennials that bloom from the first days of spring until the hard frosts of autumn.

Including plans for perennial beds, borders, islands and dooryards, *The Harrowsmith Perennial Garden* is lavishly illustrated with brilliant color photographs that will be an invaluable aid to creating your own landscapes.

160 pages
8½ x 11 inches
$17 (Save $2.95 off the published price of $19.95)

Harrowsmith Books

YES. Please send me _____ copies of *The Harrowsmith Perennial Garden* at $17 each and _____ copies of *The Harrowsmith Illustrated Book of Herbs* at $19.95 each. I enclose full payment plus $1.75 per book for shipping and handling.

Name_____

Address_____

Town_____

State_____ Zip Code_____

Place this card in an envelope together with your payment, and mail to: Harrowsmith Books, The Creamery, Charlotte, VT 05445.

SATISFACTION GUARANTEED

571

Our Favorite Herb Book

Voted the Best Garden Book of 1986 by the Garden Writers of America, *The Harrowsmith Illustrated Book of Herbs* has already been enthusiastically received by tens of thousands of readers. Their comments range from "Beautiful!" and "Inspiring" to "A great, commonsense herb book (at last)."

Author Patrick Lima tells how to design an herb garden—large, small or in containers—and gives clear advice on how to choose herbs for landscaping color, for the kitchen, for teas and fragrances. Profusely illustrated with color photographs and botanical drawings.

168 pages
8½ x 11 inches
$19.95

downward, the perianth petals flaring back like small wings. Several flowers hang from most of the 8-inch stems.

Although we give this bulb the recommended shady spot and good soil, it seldom stays more than two seasons in our garden. I suspect our winters are too much for it. But since it grows well in containers and responds to gentle forcing, the delicate flowers can be enjoyed close up indoors.

Triandrus is the parent of many hybrids, and those that we grow have proved hardy and increase freely. *Narcissus* 'Thalia' I particularly like for its white nodding flowers, like a flock of doves, several to each foot-high stem. We situated 'Thalia' behind a clump of *Erica carnea* (easiest of the heathers and one of the few species that will tolerate our nonacidic soil). When the daffodils are out and for some time after, its evergreen branches are lined with small mauve bells.

Many daffodils, wild or tame, are fragrant. Some exhale a rough, earthy scent; others are quite sweet. Best of all, to my nose, is the perfume of jonquils. Fragrance is hard to describe, and this is no exception. I can only say, plant a few bulbs of *Narcissus jonquilla*, and you are in for a spring treat.

Jonquils open after the other species have come and gone—mid-May here—and last for weeks in good condition. The waxy flowers, clustered in twos and threes at the top of 8-inch stems, are bright yellow throughout, as round as pennies, with overlapping petals behind a tiny flat cup (the source of all that sweetness). Any decent, well-drained soil will grow jonquils, and according to one expert, they "can stand a good deal of undiluted sunshine." A rock garden is a good home for them, as is the sunny side of shrubs or border edges. To please the eye as well as the nose, jonquils ought to be planted in close groups of a dozen or more. The bulbs are hardy and multiply in a way that may prompt a gardener to generosity.

As a group, wild daffodils are short—8 inches, tops—with small flowers. Most wild daffodils are out of scale with fat border perennials. They are safe, however, in a rock garden and are at home with wildflowers such as Dutchman's breeches, spring beauty, hepatica, dog's-tooth violets and bloodroot, with the caveat that the site must not be too densely shaded. Little clearings can be left in a border of primroses for a dozen bulbs of some species.

Narcissus Culture

If you have ever dug up a clump of daffodils during September in the process of reorganizing a hardy border, you'll have noticed that the bulbs are already well supplied with new white roots. It is their nature to root early in the fall, a sign that one should have daffodil bulbs in the ground as soon as possible. October planting is still on the safe side, but any later is risking failure. Be guided in planting depth by both the size of the bulbs and the nature of the soil. Generally, 4 to 6 inches of earth is enough over the round "shoulders" of most daffodil bulbs, although the smallest species go only 2 or 3 inches deep, while the very long-necked sorts and the largest bulbs of the biggest trumpet daffodils go down 6 or 9 inches. For all types, relatively deeper planting is suggested in lighter soils and shallower planting in heavy ground. And remember to allow each bulb space to multiply; 6 to 8 inches between them is not too much. The effect will be a lit-

Forget-Me-Not

tle spotty the first spring, but after a few seasons, each bulb will yield a veritable bouquet of flowers. "Close massing"—again, the observation of Louise B. Wilder—"results in an unhappy effect not unlike a feast of scrambled eggs set for a giant."

The best soil for daffodils is loamy, nourishing and well-drained. "They delight in cool conditions," says one expert, and "on hot, starved soils, cannot thrive." Both heavy clay and light sand are improved by generous dressings of organic matter—but fresh manure is not on their diet.

Daffodils are encouragingly easy to grow. True low-maintenance plants, they are cold-tolerant, insect-proof, healthy and enduring. Nor are they overly fussy about soil and site. For instance, they can bloom through emerald green *Vinca minor*—the familiar myrtle or periwinkle—under a clump of white birches. Other ground covers and other trees, especially fruit trees, provide a fine setting for them too, if the shade is not too dense. In light woodlands, they seem at home where other plants would look out of place. They can decorate the banks of a pond or stream, provided they are out of the way of standing water.

At Larkwhistle, the perennial beds appear full to overflowing with daffodils in April and early May. A month later, however, the scene has changed: a new wave of early summer flowers has succeeded the daffodils, and the promising greenery of even later-blooming perennials is very much in evidence. The beds once again appear full but this time with different plants. At first glance, you might not guess that the garden has already yielded an abundant crop of daffodils. Traces of them have all but disappeared—a neat bit of garden magic.

The trick is to plant the bulbs in the company of later-sprouting herbaceous perennials that will ultimately grow up and out to obscure the fading bulb foliage with an umbrella of their own leaves. Suitable plants to use in conjunction with daffodils include: peonies, phlox, painted daisies, daylilies, gas plants, purple loosestrife, baptisias, tall yarrows, aconites in variety, Siberian iris (but not the bearded sorts), hostas, snakeroot, the larger artemisias and *Sedum spectabile*. These are all mid- to back-of-the-border perennials. To accomplish this kind of interplanting, we set the perennials, three or five of a kind grouped together, slightly farther apart than usual—generally a full 2 feet. We then plant daffodil bulbs about 8 inches apart in a weaving fashion among the crowns of the perennials, being careful to keep bulbs at least a hand-span from the herbaceous plants. Voilà, no ugly yellowing bulb foliage ("their last state is not as lovely as their first," as Wilder puts it) and a second crop of flowers in the same spot.

Virginia Bluebells
(*Mertensia virginica*)

Bloom: April-May
Height: 1½-2 feet
Color: blue
Needs: light shade

Daffodils are also enhanced by the company of other spring flowers. Nothing could be finer planted alongside them than Virginia bluebells, a gift to gardeners from eastern American woods. Early in spring, intriguing purple shoots sprout from chubby, blackish tubers planted the previous fall. By daffodil time, shoots have become 18-inch stems clothed with tongue-shaped, blue-green foliage. At the end of each stem, a tightly packed spiral of mauve buds gradually unfurls into a succession of bells tinted the most glorious turquoise, a blue not matched by any other flower I know. I recommend mertensia, a clear favorite with visitors, for any lightly shaded site in cool, moist earth. With us, it seeds freely. Plant mertensia tubers several inches deep; the end of the tuber with the little pointed "eyes" (next year's shoots) goes up. If you have no choice but to move this plant in years to come, September is the month.

Lungworts
(*Pulmonaria* spp)

Bloom: April-May
Height: 12 inches
Color: blue
Needs: partial shade

Several not very poetically named plants related to mertensia bring more blue to the spring garden—just the color we need to set off the prevailing scheme of yellow and white. The lungworts are enduring, easy plants for almost any soil in light shade.

Pulmonaria officinalis is the ubiquitous spotted dog of older gardens, sometimes known as Jerusalem cowslip. It grows dusty-looking greenery mottled with dots and blotches of creamy white. Typical of many family members, its buds are mauve, but the bell-shaped flowers turn gradually blue. This plant is sturdy enough to be grown as a ground cover in difficult corners and can be divided to any extent in fall to increase its scope. Clumps of daffodils will flower through it.

The jewel of this genus, however, hides under the ponderous name of *Pulmonaria angustifolia azurea*, blue lungwort. Sprays of brilliant blue, funnel-shaped flowers sway over bristly, dark green leaves that are oblong and pointed. Bring this plant together with soft yellow English primroses (*Primula vulgaris*) and white narcissus 'Thalia' for a spring picture that sparkles in filtered shade.

Forget-Me-Not
(*Myosotis alpestris*)

Bloom: May-June

Height: 8 inches
Color: blue
Needs: partial shade, moist soil

I know one gardener who is so fond of the modest blue forget-me-nots that she can't bear to root out a single one. This presents a problem, since the pretty *Myosotis alpestris* is easily the garden's most unrestrained seeder, a real self-inflicted weed. At last visit, her spring garden was alight with blue, but what happens after the forget-me-nots are gone? We are strict with this spring flower; most of the seedlings are rooted out in the course of regular weeding, with only a few left to fatten up for next year's bloom in places where we think a little blue would help the picture.

Rock Cress

(*Arabis* spp, *Aubrieta* spp)

Bloom: April-June
Height: 4-8 inches
Color: white, purple, pink, red
Needs: partial shade to full sun

For the gardener keen on decorating the early garden, there are the rock cresses, which, being fibrous-rooted, provide welcome contrast to the otherwise bulb-dominated spring palette. Arabis and aubrieta both hug the ground closely and gradually creep outward to form mats of greenery and flowers along border edges, down the small hills of a rock garden or in festoons at the top of a retaining wall.

Aubrieta thrives in fertile, well-drained earth and is far better off if it has reasonably consistent moisture. It takes to full sun or light shade, but is apt to brown badly in a damp winter. Tidy it up with a shearing, and see if the dead-looking stems aren't soon bristling with new leaves. Aubrieta sprouts quickly from seed—what else would you expect of a radish relative?—and grows into a neat green tuft the first summer. If set out firmly in its permanent home in early September, it is ready to meet spring with a bright bouquet.

Arabis is like aubrieta in all ways save that its scalloped leaves are slightly larger and greyer and its typically four-petaled flowers are usually white. Easiest of border plants to grow in any well-drained loam, it needs only a close haircut after flowering to keep it thrifty and dense. With daffodils and cowslips, it creates a fresh spring trio. Both are excellent ground covers for dryish, sunny sites, providing suitable backgrounds for the taller flowers of a gentle and colorful spring.

Fritillarias

(*Fritillaria* spp)

Bloom: late spring
Height: 3 feet
Color: red, yellow, orange
Needs: sun

Behind the tall hybrid daffodils, no plant is as striking as tall *Fritillaria imperialis*, the regally named crown imperial. At all stages, whether in or out of the ground, this plant gives off a very unflowerlike scent. The smell, which I find tolerable in the garden, is strongest just as shoots emerge in spring, and has given rise to the name "stink lily" in some quarters.

If you're lucky, you will see hungry Baltimore orioles find your fritillarias, cling to the strong stems and all but disappear into the flowers in search of nourishment.

As might be expected from such a stately plant, the grapefruit-sized bulbs

Fritillary

Anemones
(*Anemone* spp)

Bloom: April-May
Height: 8-12 inches
Color: violet, white
Needs: partial shade to full sun

Named for the Greek *anemos*, or wind (hence "windflowers"), anemones of one kind or another inhabit meadows and woodlands throughout the earth's temperate lands. Two species, so distinct that you would not guess they were related, color at daffodil time. Both are so lovely, it is hard to choose between them. First to flower is *Anemone blanda* and, specifically, the cultivar 'White Splendor'; the other is *A. pulsatilla*, the pasque flower.

We had heard that spring anemones were tricky in the north and had repeatedly planted *Anemone blanda* without so much as a rewarding leaf. But hope springs eternal. Three falls ago, we tucked a dozen brownish *blanda* tubers, like gnarled bits of wood, in a sunny square foot of ordinary sandy earth in front of some heather bushes. Luck attended us. We later read that this 6-to-

of crown imperials are larger than any others northern gardeners are apt to handle. The plant has a correspondingly large appetite. Soil of preference is a sweet loam, fattened with spongy organic matter down a foot or so. Into this nourishing stuff, they are planted 4 to 6 inches deep and a good hand-span apart. Bulbs should be planted at least 3 feet from shrubs and trees, which would rob them of necessary food. At least six hours of sunshine is essential.

8-inch-tall Grecian windflower enjoys "a good loamy soil and the twiggy protection of little bushes against the blustering winds" and that it "craves all-day sun." By chance, too, we had planted the tubers where they are covered (quite literally) by tons of snow over the winter, thus ensuring that they do not freeze and thaw repeatedly. An equivalent protective mulch is necessary in gardens where winters are cold but the snow cover is iffy. Now every spring, we welcome back the mass of shiny white, thin-petaled flowers, like the most delicate daisies, each warmed by a center of yellow stamens. Flowers last for a gratifyingly long time, despite fickle spring weather.

More certain is the pasque flower, a graceful, foot-high alpine that has settled comfortably in our garden. Finely incised leaves are silky with tiny hairs, and even the flower buds are furred. Blossoms, usually light violet but in some varieties wine-red or purple, are deep, six-petaled cups filled with contrasting yellow stamens. Each bloom sits neatly in a feathery green ruff. This plant is decorative for many weeks. The plumed seed heads that follow the flowers are sought by visitors for dried winter bouquets. The pasque flower takes to dryish, rather stiff ground in full sun. Tricky to grow from seed that is not absolutely fresh, this plant regularly crops up in nurseries. Once planted, it should be left to increase in stature and beauty; the ranging roots cannot be divided with any success.

Tulip Time

The vibrant colors of May

Tulip

CHAPTER 5

Wild tulips. The very words seem incongruous because we are accustomed to thinking of tulips as the late hybrids that fly their red and yellow flags in park beds and gardens. But the tulip was not born bold, overblown and loud; it has been bred that way, groomed and gussied by generations of hybridists. If one traces tulips back to their places of origin, one lands not in Holland but in the meadows of Turkey and Yugoslavia; on rocky Asian mountainsides; in the olive groves of France, Italy and Spain; in hot North Africa; and in the ancient land of Persia. Here, wild tulips—there are about 150 species of the genus *Tulipa*—still have a home. Far away at Larkwhistle, any that we have grown have proved to be lovely little bulbous plants that recommend themselves to gardeners keen on early color.

Ranging in height from all of 3 inches to a scant foot, wild tulips are much smaller than the Holland hybrids, but all flower weeks earlier; so while they may not create the color masses of the hybrids, they *do* flower when you most appreciate them. Size, too, is in their favor. Species tulips, as they are called, are in scale with the smallest gardens or intimate corners of larger plots where the hybrids would appear awkward. In addition, many are reliably perennial, while the big late tulips tend to deteriorate after a season or two.

Species Tulips
(*Tulipa* spp)

Bloom: May
40 Height: 3-12 inches

Color: cream, yellow, red
Needs: sun

Always the first to flower—and it may be my favorite—is *Tulipa kaufmanniana*, 8 inches tall and, quite simply, a beautiful bulb. From the center of broad, blue-green leaves, each smartly edged with a pencil line of red, emerge tapered buds that open into gold-centered, cream-colored flowers marked with a stroke of soft red on the outside of the petals. Interplanted with the small bulbs of glory-of-the-snow (*Chionodoxa* spp), the creamy tulip cups above sky blue stars make an easy spring picture anywhere in sun.

On the heels of *Tulipa kaufmanniana* come *T. turkestanica* and *T. praestans*, both multiflowered. The first carries 6 to 12 nodding, bronze-green buds on each foot-tall stem. The six-petaled starry flowers, ivory white with yellow centers, are enlivened by dark brown stamens. With us it flourishes at the edge of an ordinary flower border, even pushing its way through a cover of woolly lamb's ears (*Stachys byzantina*).

The buds of *Tulipa praestans* are little flames in the chilly spring garden. Its flowers are scarlet, "not deep, but high

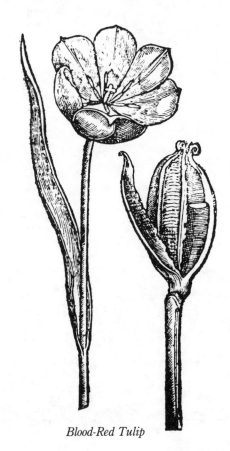

Blood-Red Tulip

and thin, a lovely flashing color," an observer once wrote. Either of these two species shows well just behind white rock cress (*Arabis albida*). Nearby might grow orange and yellow cowslips (*Primula veris*), one of the few primroses that, given decent soil, will thrive in the sunny spots that wild tulips need.

Variations on a tulip theme continue with the appearance of *Tulipa tarda* (sometimes listed as *T. dasystemon*), a sprightly small thing, generous with its annually increasing clusters of 2-inch white and yellow flowers that open flat and starry from deceptively dowdy buds. This tiny Turk reaches all of 3 inches, but in a few seasons, a dozen bulbs form a continuous band of white and gold down a rock garden slope or along a border edge.

Little *Tulipa linifolia* is a gemlike species with ruby cups that flare widely in the spring sun. We smothered this 6-inch mite under a dense cover of sedum, and it gradually disappeared—a lesson learned. In general, however, delicate, shallow-rooted plants growing over the bulbs are a comfort and protection for wild tulips; try sedum, creeping thyme, pussytoes or flat mats of *Veronica repens*.

The 8-inch *Tulipa chrysantha* repeats (but softly) the red and yellow coloring of many big late tulips. *Tulipa clusiana*, the lady tulip, is one of the few wild tulips that also have a common name. Its slender, crimson and white buds open into elegant white flowers with a wine-dark center.

The rounded flowers of *Tulipa sylvestris*, copper in the bud but deep yellow when open, smell like sweet violets.

Two pink species, *Tulipa pulchella* and *T. saxatilis*, sprout from between flat stones that pave our front porch. Somehow, the tulips, as well as the dwarf columbines, thymes and bellflowers that share its porch space, are nourished by sun, sand and stone.

Finally, we come to two species that prepare us for the imminent parade of hybrid tulips. Both species have been tampered with by gene jugglers and show it. *Fosterana* 'Red Emperor' is as flushed and angry as Lewis Carroll's Queen of Hearts. Catalogues wax ecstatic in describing this "brilliant, dazzling scarlet giant, larger than any other tulip." *Greigii* hybrids will also "ignite your garden with flame-red bloom." Once, we planted them, but when they flowered, everything else in the garden

seemed to pale—or cringe. Who wants some red-faced tyrant dominating the gentle spring show? I'll wait for the Oriental poppies to provide the razzle-dazzle.

Species Tulip Care

Early fall planting is not necessary for wild tulips and may even be detrimental. November is the month to tuck them in place. They do best with deeper planting than most small bulbs; a full 4 inches of soil should top the little bulbs of *tarda*, *pulchella*, *linifolia* and the like, while 8 inches down is not too deep for *kaufmanniana* and *praestans*. In the matter of soil, wild tulips are not fastidious. Although one expert recommends "a rather heavy soil, rich in humus," they make do nicely in our light, sandy loam. Swift drainage, in any case, is essential; in damp earth, surround the bulbs with a cushion and cover of sand.

All wild tulips crave a place in the sun, and none like strong-growing neighbors to blanket them in shadow. A sunny rock garden is the perfect home for them, but we grow the largest species at the edges of perennial beds and smaller sorts at the base of edging rocks or in intimate corners of the garden with alpine gentians, edelweiss, the lowest thymes and other scaled-down plants.

Hybrid Tulips

Bloom: May
Height: 18 inches
Color: red, yellow, pink, white
Needs: full sun, neutral soil

I am of two minds about hybrid tulips. After the quiet hues of daffodils and other early flowers, I welcome, with reservations, the bold and varied colors that tulips add to the spring picture. Although I concede that tulips play an important role in the May scene, my enthusiasm for them is not unbounded. I still associate them with formal beds and stiff, uninspired plantings.

But perhaps my biggest grudge against tulips has to do with their lack of health. For all their bold looks, tulips fall easy prey to several fungal diseases that curtail their stay in the garden. Although a number of cultivars have remained hale and sound at Larkwhistle for as long as five years, in most gardens, tulips simply refuse to settle in for a long run. This means that gardeners who want to include them with other perennials in a Maytime composition must be continually rethinking and renovating the picture.

For all of that, we still succumb to the blandishments of catalogues and plant a few dozen new bulbs each fall. No other flower of the season can match the tulip's color range. Few are as tall; at a season when dwarf perennials predominate, tulips lift the color above ground level and take the eye from dwarf border plants up to that old apple tree blossoming pink against the blue spring sky.

The early and midseason sorts are a prelude to the full May symphony of tall Darwin, cottage and lily-flowered tulips. Pink cultivars such as 'Esther,' 'Rosy Wings' and 'Smiling Queen' and the lavender-blue sorts are lovely in the company of bleeding hearts, blue intermediate iris and many of the spring border plants, save for acid-yellow alyssums. With the alyssum, we grow 'Dillenburg,' a very late tulip shaded like a ripe peach; the delicate lemon and cream of 'Sweet Harmony' would do here too. Ivory-colored and egg-shaped 'Maureen' fits in anywhere but is especially effective tucked into a quiet corner of green and silver foliage and white flowers.

Hybrid Tulip Care

Fall is the time to tuck tulips in place, and late rather than early is the recommendation. The bulbs can be set aside in a cool, dry place until as late as December (provided the earth is not frozen), while you get daffodils, crocuses, lilies and the rest into the ground. For tulips, the ground ought to be loamy, sweet and well-drained. A dusting of crushed limestone should be dug into acidic soil to raise the pH to neutral or just above. Tulips do well in rather heavy soil that has been loosened somewhat with well-decayed organic matter; fresh manure is definitely not to their liking.

Tulips need a place in the sun. In shade, they stretch and bend in a valiant effort to see the light. Here, we plant them in sunny perennial borders in oval groups of 10 or 20 bulbs, each about 6 inches from the next. If the

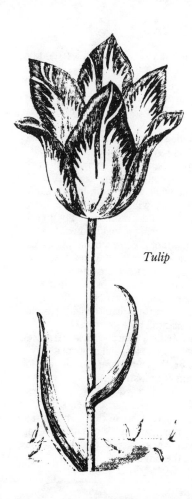

Tulip

bulbs are tucked close by clumps of *Sedum spectabile*, daylilies or silver-leaved yarrows, these perennials will soon grow up and out to conceal fading tulip leaves and renew color in that same spot.

The recommended planting depth moves up and down according to whom one hears or reads. Tulips have a remarkable ability to push their way through as much as 12 inches of soil. Some experts suggest that this very deep planting helps keep tulips in the garden years longer, providing there is plenty of rich soil beneath the bulbs. We have tried deep planting and find that, yes, bulbs stay healthy for a season or two more, but when the inevitable decline comes and they must be lifted, they are that much harder to get at. Now, we plant tulips about 6 inches deep, count on them for two or three seasons, then dig them up and toss them out when the flowers grow few or small and the foliage shows signs of spotty fungus. If we want to put fresh tulips back in that same spot, we dig out a bushel or two of soil and replace it with fresh rich earth from the vegetable garden. Once the flowers are spent, tulip leaves must be left to yellow and ripen thoroughly, in the process feeding the bulbs that will produce next spring's flowers.

Spring Edgings

Tulips show their real worth in garden pictures when they are planted not in the splendid isolation of a separate bed but in association with other spring perennials, flowering shrubs or blossoming trees. In our garden, they are allowed to break rank and congregate in informal groups here and there in the mixed borders. For example, in May, several dwarf perennials are in full bloom along the border edges. Behind each mat of creeping phlox or each cushion of dwarf catnip, 10 to 15 tulips are planted in a close colony.

Candytuft
(*Iberis sempervirens*)

Bloom: May-June
Height: 8-12 inches
Color: white
Needs: full sun

If it flowered in colors other than

43

white, perennial candytuft would rival creeping phlox as the best spring edging. Here is a little bush (8 to 12 inches tall and, eventually, 18 inches or more across) that is presentable year-round. Spring thaw sees the small, narrow leaves still dark green and fresh. By late May, the foliage is obscured by a mass of chalk-white flowers. After an early summer shearing, the plants lapse into neat green again. If foliage should become brown or shrivel in a damp, snowless winter, a spring trim will encourage fresh growth.

Candytuft can be raised easily from seed. Give seedlings at least a foot between them, and in a season or two, they will grow together. Although not picky about the soil it grows in, candytuft does need a warm, sunny spot where water drains away quickly.

Creeping Phlox

(*Phlox subulata*)

Bloom: May-June
Height: 4-6 inches
Color: blue, pink, white
Needs: full sun

44 Perhaps the most effective of spring edgings is creeping phlox, also commonly called ground phlox, moss phlox or moss pink. Its greenery is narrow and pointed, a mass of little needlelike leaves that appear prickly but are soft to the touch.

Garden-bred phlox vary in habit of growth. Some are loose, lax and springy, others close and compact like dense green mosses, but none grows taller than 6 inches. Flowers range through all shades of pink, to white, to a lovely silvery lavender best described as "moonlit blue." Few perennials are as floriferous; for three or four weeks in late spring, phlox stems are hidden under countless crowding flowers—flat, round as a penny and formed of five notched petals—equally effective edging a flower bed, covering a stretch of sunny ground or cascading over a wall top or down a rock garden slope.

Once planted, creeping phlox requires minimal attention, only a single close shearing of foliage once the spring flower show is over—no watering, no spraying, no coddling.

Seed will not grow the named varieties, but a single nursery plant, after it has been growing in the garden for a season or two, can be turned into any number of new ones. Here's how: Like many ground-hugging plants, phlox fans out from its center on laterally moving shoots that eventually put down roots of their own. This natural layering process can be encouraged and hastened if the little side branches are held snugly to the earth with a small stone or hairpin and some soil is firmed over the contact point. Layer 10 or 20 shoots while you're at it. In two months or so, roots will have formed. Snip the layers from the mother plant with scissors, and using a small trowel, ease them out of the ground and plant them firmly and immediately in a new locale. For a more immediate effect from this deliberate grower, I like to plant a half-dozen shoots, set about 4 inches apart, in a close group that I consider as one new plant. Three groups spaced a foot apart make a generous drift. Creeping phlox take to any soil short of soggy; rich earth is not a prerequisite, but lots of sun is a must. If after some years plants tend to grow leggy and leafless along the lower part of their stems, sift some sandy loam or fine compost right over them, and work this material into the network of criss-crossing branches with the fingers.

Early Iris
(*Iris* spp)

Bloom: May-June
Height: 10-28 inches
Color: every color
Needs: full sun

June is the month for iris, but weeks before the parade of gorgeous, tall bearded iris arrives, scaled-down versions, called dwarf (10 to 15 inches tall) and intermediate (15 to 28 inches tall), wave advance flags. Like the tall bearded iris in all ways save size, the dwarfs and intermediates move along on expanding rhizomes and produce the typical fleur-de-lis. The shorter iris are self-supporting (in contrast to the taller, which usually need a prop), drought-resistant, exceedingly hardy perennials that soon increase to form pools of clear color in the May garden. Their reduced stature makes them suitable for smaller gardens, and their early flowering extends the iris season in gardens where there is room for all kinds.

The shorter the iris, the earlier it flowers. Dwarfs come first, often blooming with the daffodils. The inter-mediates are in sync with tulips, and the two set each other off uncommonly well in both form and color—sky blue iris with pink tulips, dark purple iris with yellow tulips or any mix that takes your fancy. Colors range from white, cream and yellow through peach and orange to almost red, and there are many shades of blue, lavender and violet.

All of the bearded iris, early or late, require a sunny site and swift drainage. Otherwise, they are adaptable and need only a bit of tidying—removal of spotty leaves and spent flower stalks—in summer and division when the rhizomes start to crawl all over each other and flowers grow sparse. A few weeks after flowering is the right time for division.

Leopard's Bane
(*Doronicum* spp)

Bloom: April-May
Height: 1½-3 feet
Color: yellow
Needs: full sun to partial shade

Leopard's bane, the first of the garden's daisies to bloom, is an easy perennial whose deep yellow flowers and 3-foot height are appreciated at a time

Great Leopard's Bane

45

when low plants and soft colors predominate.

Leopard's bane—the name comes from a legend that leopard hunters once dipped their arrowheads in juice pressed from its roots—responds to decent soil but makes the best of the less-than-perfect stuff. In addition, this hardy plant can be set in either full sun or fairly dense shade any time, spring to fall, and divides more easily than most. A single plant looks a little forlorn and weedy, but a massed group, say, 3 feet long and 2 feet across, will light any dim garden corner.

Dwarf Catnip
(*Nepeta* × *faassenii*)

Bloom: June-August
Height: 12-18 inches
Color: lavender-blue
Needs: full sun

Much less showy than phlox, but useful for variety and misty blue accents among brighter flowers, is a decorative dwarf form of catnip called *Nepeta* × *faassenii* (listed in old gardening books and some current catalogues as *N. mus-sinii*). Early each spring, this easy-care, drought-resistant perennial sprouts a fresh crop of fragrant, pebbled gray-green leaves. By tulip time, there are lots of slender foot-high stems set with many small lavender-blue flowers, like mint blossoms magnified. I like single specimens of this neat, mounding plant at regular intervals along a border edge, with a dozen pink, pale yellow or crimson tulips behind each.

Bleeding Hearts
(*Dicentra* spp)

Bloom: May-June
Height: 2½-3 feet
Color: pink-and-white
Needs: partial shade

Few plants are as glorious in May as well-grown clumps of bleeding heart (*Dicentra spectabilis*), their arching stems hung with fanciful deep pink and white hearts, like some exotic confection, above elegantly divided blue-green foliage.

Here is a neat, minimal-care, long-lived 3-foot plant for many sites, sunny or shaded, formal or natural. I like to set single clumps, just back of front, at intervals in a mixed border, with tulips and early dwarf perennials for company. Bleeding hearts can be used as accents on either side of a path or doorway or in woodland or semiwild gardens where ferns and wildflowers live.

Bleeding hearts grow from pronged, tan-colored rhizomes, not unlike peony rootstocks. Like peonies, too, these roots are planted in the fall, their season of dormancy. Handle the brittle roots gingerly to avoid snapping them. Alternatively, actively growing (sometimes even flowering) potted plants can be found in nurseries in spring and can be set out, soil and all. The initial work of turning a half-bushel or so of decayed manure, compost and/or peat moss into the earth for each plant will be rewarded with stronger growth and more flowers over a longer time. In seasons to come, an organic mulch will maintain moisture and fertility. Since a large part of this plant's charm comes from its graceful, fountainlike form, I suggest a spacing of 1½ to 2 feet between clumps or an unplanted area 2½ feet wide around a single specimen, so that plants can arch out naturally. Keep tall, flopping perennials such as anchusas or

Columbine

delphiniums—unless they are conscientiously staked—well away from bleeding hearts. Another tip: Bleeding heart foliage, lovely as it is in spring, dies away by midsummer. If a plant of baby's-breath occupies the space behind, the misty veil of its bloom can be drawn over the bare space.

Columbines
(*Aquilegia* spp)

Bloom: April-May
Height: 1½-3 feet
Color: red-and-yellow, purple, pink, yellow, white, blue
Needs: partial shade to full sun

The first time I saw clumps of soaring columbines blooming in a city front yard—this was years before I had a garden of my own—I was completely taken with the flowers, with how the petals, spurs and sepals fit together like an artfully wrought puzzle. Since then, it's been my pleasure to grow many clumps of columbines, many kinds and colors, but I am still smitten.

Many perennials we buy as started plants, but columbines we always raise from seed, for several reasons. First, they are so easy that any gardener who has seen parsley or broccoli through these steps has the patience and know-how to achieve a fine crop of columbines. Second, seeds open the door to a wider world of columbine beauty. Finally, they are lovelier in groups of three, five or more, and a $1.50 packet of seeds will grow at least $15 worth of plants. Columbines commonly do not live more than three seasons in the garden, so we keep a batch of new plants coming along from seed to replace any that succumb to stem borers—columbine enemy number one with us—or winter.

Columbine seeds are shiny and black and not too small. April is the month to sow them; indoors is the place to start. To grow, say, six each of the red and gold and of the blue and white 'Olympias'—if you get the lot from seed to full flowering, you can pat yourself on the back, enjoy the compliments and marvel at the blossoms—you'll need two 8-inch bulb pots (shorter and broader-based than ordinary flowerpots) filled with the porous medium described in chapter 2 and two packs of seed, which you are advised to chill in the refrigerator for five days. At seeding time, do not cover the seeds, but simply press them lightly into the soil surface. Space the 15 or so seeds several inches apart; you'll want to keep every seedling that sprouts. Water the pots from beneath, and drape a piece of clear plastic (or use a pane of glass) over them. Set pots in a warm place, but not in full sun. In several weeks, little green backs will show through the earth. Remove the plastic or glass, set the pots in a very sunny window, and see that seedlings stay moist—but not sodden—as they grow.

When the seedlings have sent up five or six small ferny leaves, the time has come for the move outdoors. Lift seedlings carefully out of the pot—an ordinary dinner fork or teaspoon is a good tool for the job—and set them firmly, a full foot apart, in the friable earth of a nursery bed or, even better, in a sheltering cold frame fitted with a slatted shade. Pick an overcast day for the move, and if several days of cloud and showers follow, so much the better. In any case, some artificial shade is a help for a few days.

Once they take hold, the seedlings should shoot up over summer. Fertilizer will fatten the clumps, of course. In early September, they are lifted once more with as many roots intact as possible—this time you'll need a shovel—and set out in their permanent places. I like to dig oversized transplanting holes in the border and stir a spadeful of crumbly manure or compost deeply into each before lowering in the columbine. Backfill with earth firmed around the roots, and water generously to settle the works. Columbines thrive in earth that contains enough organic matter to stay nicely moist and well-textured. "It is not generally realized how cruelly [they] suffer in dry weather," says one expert, who also recommends liberal watering during drought. A leaf or straw mulch is useful. Plants should grow 12 to 18 inches apart. Sun or partial shade is all the same to them, provided the earth is fertile and moist.

Jacob's Ladder
(*Polemonium* spp)

Bloom: May-June
Height: 2½ feet
Color: blue
Needs: partial shade to full sun

In an arbor-shaded raised bed flanking our door-side herb garden, columbines grow next to Jacob's ladder, whose common name refers to the precisely ascending arrangement of the leaflets. Jacob's ladder is among the first perennials to sprout in spring. Its greenery, fresh, dense and tidy, lasts in good condition the summer through and is in large measure a reason for the plant's appeal. The 3-foot stems, upright and self-supporting, are each topped by clustered flower buds that open successively over six to eight weeks into pretty, 1-inch, sky-blue cups sparked with yellow stamens. A single plant makes little impact, but four or five in a group—planted a foot apart—create a haze of blue in any lightly shaded place.

Jacob's ladder grows best in the fertile, humusy soil that suits columbines and bleeding hearts; it is also well-placed with hostas and ferns.

Yellow Fumitory
(*Corydalis lutea*)

Bloom: May-August
Height: 12 inches

Color: yellow
Needs: partial shade to full sun

No better companion for Jacob's ladder could be found than a foreplanting of *Corydalis lutea*. Kin to the Dutchman's breeches of northern woods, corydalis has similarly dainty foliage, gray-green, much divided and fernlike. But there its daintiness ends. The plant is vigorous and quick and more generous with its dangling clusters of yellow flowers than any other perennial I know—literally nonstop blossoms from May until September. Corydalis likes to get a foothold in a dry-built stone wall, and if given free rein, this rampant seeder will completely veil the wall in feathery foliage and flowers in a few seasons. A good perennial, this, sun- or shade-tolerant and showy.

Violets

(*Viola* spp)

Bloom: *April-September*
Height: 3-12 inches
Color: every color
Needs: partial shade to full sun

Almost every garden grows a crop of violas of one kind or another, usually bold-faced, multicolored pansies, hybrids of *Viola tricolor*, bought in bloom every May. But there is a host of other violas, both garden-bred and wild, to color spring days. Not unlike pansies, but prettier to my eye (not so big and blotchy), are cultivars of *V. cornuta*. These we count on for a long-lasting ribbon of color—white, yellow, apricot, rusty red and, best of all, clear blue— along the edge of a lightly shaded primrose border. With generous soil preparation at the start, a few deep drinks during drought and removal of withered flowers, these violas carry on flowering all summer. As often as not, the plants survive winter and resume blooming in spring if last year's straggly stems are snipped back to the tufts of fresh green.

Viola cornuta and *V. tricolor* cultivars are very easy to raise from seeds, a project worth undertaking if you want plants in quantity. The timing, however, is a little different from most. Mid-August is the time we sow short rows of seeds and when the weather turns chilly in late September, we cover the frame with its storm window sash to keep things summery under the glass for a while longer, but come November,

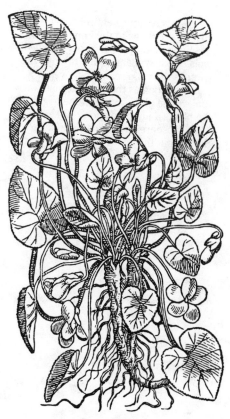

Sweet Violet

49

the sash is removed entirely to accustom seedlings to the impending winter. Snow-blanketed or straw-mulched, viola or pansy plants come through the winter green and ready to flower.

Just as soon as the snow is gone, we replace the glass on the frame to give the plants a jump on spring. By early May, most are showing a first flower. Setting out the violas has become part of our spring ritual.

If *Viola cornuta* and *V. tricolor* cultivars are best grown as biennials, other members of the genus are hardy perennials that take to the most northerly gardens. *V. odorata*, the sweet-scented violet of English gardens and spring nosegays, flowers profusely in shady places and then flings hardy seeds far and wide. It can be a (lovely) pest, as can Johnny-jump-ups (*V. tricolor*), a sassy small viola that will stretch (or jump) right through a peony, if it happens to lodge underneath one, in an effort to see the sun. A good carpet for daffodils, tulips or lilies, purple and gold Johnnies flower blithely from spring thaw to snowfall. Start this one from seed once, and it will stay in and around the garden ever after. But be warned, it can cause some confusion in a perennial border if you are keen on every plant in its allotted place.

The June Garden

Poppies, peonies and iris hit their stride

Poppy

CHAPTER 6

It is easy to have a beautiful garden in June," one expert gardener has written. The days grow steadily longer and warmer, frosts are over, and gentle rains fall often; everything, in fact, conspires to accelerate growth and spur flowering. Whatever pests and problems may be in store for us in July and August, the solstice garden is generally fresh and flowery, a fulfillment of earlier promise and a gift to hardworking gardeners.

The June garden was the first to re-

51

Opium Poppy

pay us at Larkwhistle. My partner and I had worked for four seasons digging borders, forking out quack grass roots, turning under manure and decayed leaves and hauling limestone rocks to raise and define the planting spaces. We had been reading about perennials in treasured turn-of-the-century gardening books and scouring catalogues and nurseries for seeds and plants. With paper planning, a fair bit of on-site impromptu planting and some subsequent rearranging, the garden took shape.

Iris set out in two 5-by-30-foot beds gave a smattering of bloom the first year, an encouraging hint of what we could expect. As the seasons turned, the perennials fattened up to fill their allotted spaces—and sometimes more. The garden was maturing. And then, quite suddenly one June morning (or so it seems in memory), we awoke to find flower borders brimming with blossoms.

I wanted to shout, "Perfect! Stay just as you are." But, alas, as one gardener has observed, "The wretched plants will not stand still." The flowers that bloom on either side of the summer solstice came and went, leaving gaps where there had been loveliness and sending us back to the books and out to other gardens in search of follow-up perennials. But we had seen the magic that June can work with a gardener's helping hand.

Oriental Poppies
(*Papaver orientale*)

Bloom: June
Height: 3-4 feet
Color: red, pink, orange, white
Needs: full sun

Whatever the calendar says, I always think that summer starts when the first Oriental poppy bursts its furry bud. There is nothing quite so spectacular as the big flaunting flowers of *Papaver orientale* tottering on yard-high stems; the four-petaled crepe-textured cups, a hand-span across, are filled with quivering purple-black stamens that give way to little pepper shaker pods dispensing poppy seeds to the winds.

In the garden, these brilliant things must be placed more carefully if they are not to dominate the scene. At Larkwhistle, scarlet Oriental poppies accompany cream-colored bearded iris and blue anchusas or mingle with the ferny greenery and white lace caps of sweet cicely (*Myrrhis odorata*).

But in other parts of the garden, pink cultivars of *Papaver orientale* steal the show. These were new to me some years ago and continue to surprise visitors who only know the red. 'Betty Ann' is as pink as an old-fashioned rose; 'Cheerio's' light pink petals are marked at their base with a blotch the color of Bing cherries. Either combines beautifully with blue, lavender or inky violet bearded iris and pink or crimson coral bells. Set a plant of lacy valerian behind and an edging of silver-leaved lamb's ears in front, and you have a picture to satisfy any gardener's soul.

Keep in mind that they are an ephemeral lot, here for a few weeks, then gone. Even their foliage is fleeting. By midsummer, it has disappeared underground, leaving no trace of former glory —leaving, in fact, a gap in the border, unless we have thought to plant other perennials fore and aft of the poppies to mask their defection. Baby's-breath, showy stonecrop, heleniums, late-blooming daylilies and several of the taller yarrows are useful for that job.

Oriental poppies have a nap during July and August, then wake up and sprout new leaves during cool, damp fall days. The time to move them is in late summer, just as they show above ground. Like peonies and gas plants, they are among the perennials that can stay put, undisturbed, for decades. But to increase a favorite cultivar, gently dig up a clump when you see a start of new growth. Likely, the earth will fall away from the thonglike roots. Then, using your fingers and a small, sharp knife and being careful not to snap the brittle roots, split the clustered shoots into one- or two-crowned divisions. Plant these right away, firmly and at least a foot apart, with the juncture of leaves and roots 2 inches below ground level. Water to firm the soil, then hope that the roots take hold. In my experience, Oriental poppies are practically indestructible once established, but more reluctant than other perennials to settle in at first.

Bearded Iris

(*Iris* spp)

Bloom: May-June
Height: 9 inches - 4 feet
Color: every color
Needs: full sun

From early spring until well into July, iris of one kind or another are in bloom. And June is the month for tall bearded iris and Siberian iris to shine. Each type has specific requirements, and each fills a different niche in the landscape.

Bearded iris, highly bred and exceedingly fancy, have been derived over decades from crosses between three faithful "flags" of old gardens: *Iris germanica*, *I. pallida* and *I. florentina*, source of the herbal fixative orrisroot, which is much used in potpourris and perfumery.

Clearly, the June garden picture would lose much of its sparkle without bearded iris. All of our sunny flower borders have a core group or two of iris, their colors chosen to complement the perennials blooming with them.

Iris Care

"What are you planting those for?" a visiting friend asked one July morning as he watched us tucking iris rhizomes into a new border. "You'll never get rid of them." Iris have an unfair reputation for spreading their fat rootstocks be-

Double-Bearing Iris

yond control. In truth, they are no quicker to increase than many other perennials and much easier to check than some; invasive they are not. Besides, if you are growing some of the showier sorts, you'll have a list of fellow gardeners waiting for any excess.

Bearded iris sprout fans of flat, blue-green sword-shaped leaves from elongated rhizomes, which are thickened underground stems, rather than from roots. The actual roots, thin, white and very tough, spread down and out from both sides of the rhizome—which gives us a clue about planting iris. For each rhizome, trowel out two holes (rather than one), side by side and about 4 inches deep with a narrow ridge of earth between them. Set a rhizome on the ridge with roots parted naturally into the holes, then backfill with soil firmed over the roots and just covering the rhizome. A few rain showers will wash some soil away to expose the tan backs for the sun-baking they need for health.

Midsummer is the time to set out new iris. Mail-order roots generally arrive in August, but if one is dividing from the garden, July (or several weeks after the current crop of flowers) is a better time.

Nurseries usually send single rhizomes with a short fan of leaves. For best effect, I prefer to set three to seven rhizomes of one color, 10 inches apart, in an oval group with fans turned outward to avoid later crowding. In narrow borders (3 to 5 feet wide), such groups could alternate with single plants of late-blooming perennials such as daylilies, lythrums or yellow yarrows, which provide not only contrast in plant form to the stiff iris swords, but also give color in July and August. In a wider border, low pinks, sedums, thymes or coral bells could run along the edge. For a sunny site, just a few plantings are easier to maintain.

In untended gardens, old clumps of bearded iris often grow merrily on from year to year, but like most plants, they are better for a little care. Sun is essential, at least six hours a day. See, too, that the soil is well drained and sweetened with lime if necessary. Soil texture is less important—light or heavy loam is much the same to iris—but soggy spots are fatal.

Care includes the removal of badly spotted or withered brown leaves from the outside of the fans once or twice during the summer and the clearing of debris from the rhizomes so that they can breathe and sunbathe. I have never sprayed iris for anything, nor do I intend to start. In the fall, scissor the leaves back to 3-inch fans to avoid a major spring cleanup of soggy leaves. Thus nurtured, a collection of tall bearded iris will bring a rainbow of color in June.

Siberian Iris
(*Iris sibirica*)

Bloom: June-July
Height: 3 feet
Color: blue, purple, red, white
Needs: full sun to partial shade

Quite different from bearded iris in terms of foliage, flowers and needs, Siberian iris are extremely hardy, fibrous-rooted perennials that soon form stout clumps of elegant leaves — thin, reedy, dark green and gracefully arched — topped by fleurs-de-lis colored conservatively in shades of blue, lavender and white. They luxuriate in moist, fertile ground and even in fairly wet sites. Ordinary garden soil usually requires the addition of peat moss, decayed manure, compost or rotted leaves — but not lime. A leaf mulch (provided you are not plagued by slugs) helps retain both fertility and moisture.

A noninvasive habit of clumping and persistently good foliage make Siberian iris appropriate for important focal or accent points in the garden, alternating with hostas at regular intervals along a shaded path or on either side of an entrance to the house. Their healthy constitution and height recommend them for the middle sections of low-maintenance perennial borders where they can be interplanted with daffodils for spring color.

Pinks & Sweet William
(*Dianthus* spp)

Bloom: May-June
Height: 4-12 inches
Color: pink, white, red
Needs: full sun, alkaline soil

As the flower gardener's year moves along, certain colors tend to predominate for a while and then give way to others. Much of June's rosy glow is provided by pinks, species of dianthus valued both for their neat mounds of silver or green foliage and their extravagant crop of spice-scented flowers. Our garden suits pinks to a tee: the soil is warm, sweet, sandy and quick to drain, and the site is fully open to the sun. Dianthus gives up in cold, heavy or waterlogged ground and steadfastly refuses to grow in shade.

Although we have grown about a dozen species of dianthus over the years, four stand out from the rest for beauty, hardiness, ease of culture and suitability for general border use. *Dianthus caesius*, the spicy 6-inch Cheddar pink said to decorate the white cliffs of Dover in silver and rose, is equally comfortable hanging from a chink in a sunny rock wall or sprawling over the edge of a flower bed. *D. arenarius*, a white pink, sends up hundreds of flat, fringed flowers, like scented snowflakes, above its short turf of green. Mats of this excellent edging plant have lived for eight years along an iris border, with only the attention of a short haircut after flowering and a top dressing of crumbly loam worked in among the leaves every few years if the plants

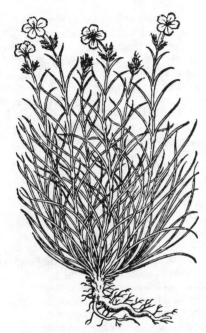

White Mountain Pink

Sweet William

Very nearly indestructible, the maiden pink (*Dianthus deltoides*) seeds with weedlike abandon and can be used as a ground cover or edging. Its leaves are dark green and dense below smallish flowers of a most piercing, almost neon crimson. This is the only dianthus I know of that lacks scent.

Few plants make such dramatic drifts of clear color as sweet William, *Dianthus barbatus*, an old-fashioned biennial available also in cultivars such as 'Newport Pink,' 'Scarlet' and the wine-dark 'Crimson Velvet.' (The dwarf "wee willies" and annual midgets are not as effective.)

Quite easy to grow from seed, sweet William is worth including in perennial gardens. It is sown indoors in April or outdoors by mid-May. Plants are grown over summer, 12 inches apart, in a nursery bed where they develop into strong, leafy rosettes ready to go into their flowering quarters in September. Next June, and probably well into July, they will shoot up 18-inch stems topped by flattish flower heads—like exotic broccoli—of rose, red or blackish crimson. Three or more clumps set just back of the front of a border make a solid band of color.

show patchy spots.

Then there is *Dianthus allwoodii*, a garden-bred strain that fringes one of our borders with silver and seems to explode into fireworks of fragrant flowers—in shades of pink and crimson, single-toned or dark on light, pennyround or fringed, single or double—to celebrate the summer solstice. Take cuttings for spring replacements.

Pyrethrums

(Chrysanthemum coccineum)

Bloom: June-July
Height: 2 feet
Color: pink, red, white, lavender
Needs: full sun

All through June, clusters of pink and crimson pyrethrums, or painted daisies, sway in the borders with spice-scented dianthus in front and a flock of blue Siberian iris fluttering behind.

Among the most steadfast, useful and care-free of perennials, pyrethrums sprout quickly from seed (within three weeks), develop in one season into flowering-sized clumps and return more strongly in seasons to come. If necessary, they can be propagated by root division in early spring, just as new leaves appear. Fertile loam well supplied with nourishing organic matter grows the best painted daisies; they resent dry ground and respond to thorough watering or mulch with a fuller crop of showy, long-lasting flowers. Nothing could be finer for early summer bouquets. Plant a few clumps in the vegetable garden for cut flowers.

Flax Flowers

(Linum perenne)

Bloom: May-August
Height: 2 feet
Color: blue
Needs: full sun

More blue for June comes from the pretty flax flowers of *Linum perenne*, an 18-inch plant as delicate and airy as anchusa is large and sprawling. In a flower bed, perennial flax serves to lighten more massive and complicated flowers such as peonies and iris, much as baby's-breath does in a bouquet of roses.

Perennial flax sprouts quickly from seed scattered in the garden. Young plants are thinned to 8 inches between them. Seeds sown outdoors in late spring will yield flowers 12 months later, but impatient gardeners might seed indoors in March – 3-inch peat pots are suitable containers – for first-season bloom.

Linum will make itself at home in any sunny corner, lodging among the iris rhizomes, at the edges of paths or wherever the feathery seedlings get a roothold in well-drained earth.

Cornflowers

(Centaurea montana)

Bloom: May-July
Height: 2 feet
Color: blue
Needs: full sun

Many gardeners know cornflowers or bachelor's buttons as easy 3-foot annuals that grow quickly from May-sown seed and decorate the garden for a single summer with fluffy round flowers so distinctly blue that they have given their name to a shade of that color – cornflower blue. Less fleeting and not quite as vivid is a perennial counterpart, *Centaurea montana*, known commonly as the mountain bluet or, simply, perennial cornflower.

Perennial cornflowers look best set in groups of three or more – a single plant makes little show – just back of front in company with poppies, iris of any color, dianthus and the like. Since they spread from both roots and seeds, they might be left out of smaller gardens in favor of something showier and more stay-at-home; but our traveling bachelor's buttons are a good choice for next-to-no-maintenance flower beds that could include Siberian iris, daylilies and rose loosestrife for later color.

Foxgloves
(*Digitalis* spp)

Bloom: June-July
Height: 3-8 feet
Color: cream, yellow, pink, red
Needs: partial shade, acid soil

In all my gardening days, I doubt that any crop of flowers has given me as much pride and joy as last year's 8-foot-tall 'Excelsior' foxgloves hung thickly with darkly freckled cream, yellow, pink or magenta tubular or finger-shaped (hence, digitalis) flowers. They were spectacular towering behind old rosebushes billowing with bloom, with the June sky for a backdrop.

If only they would come back every year. But, being biennial, foxgloves, like sweet William, grow a rosette of greenery one year, flower the next and then, after scattering their tiny seeds, disappear. Wise are the gardeners who avail themselves of some of the many seedlings left behind. These can be tucked into a corner of the vegetable garden to fatten up in fertile soil and then, come early September, lifted carefully and transferred to a flower bed for next year's color. Seed is a better way to bring foxgloves into the garden initially, and the method described for anchusas, below, will do as well for digitalis.

Given their woodland origins, foxgloves grow to greater heights in a home garden if the earth is humus-rich and moist; compost, leaf mold, peat moss and old manure all help. Although foxgloves thrive in shade, they also do well in sun in our coolish garden.

Anchusa
(*Anchusa italica*)

Bloom: June-August
Height: 3 feet
Color: blue
Needs: full sun

All of June's rosiness needs complementary blue, and few plants wear the color as well as anchusa. In fact, "no plant," according to one old-time writer, "not excepting the delphiniums, decks itself in a more truly azure color." A seldom-grown 4-foot perennial, *Anchusa italica*, or *A. azurea* — its common names include Italian bugloss and alkanet — shows its family ties to both borage and comfrey in rather coarse, rough, hairy leaves and stems and spiraled clusters of mauve buds that unfurl into five-petaled blue blossoms.

Nurseries seem to ignore this showy plant, but anchusa is not difficult to grow from seeds. Listed as a biennial in some catalogues, anchusa is more accurately a short-lived perennial, in the manner of columbines, flax or Iceland poppies; in our garden, it usually reappears for three or four years. But if older clumps deteriorate in the end, there are always seedlings left behind — sometimes far too many — that can be lifted when still fairly small and transplanted toward the back of flower beds, perhaps behind pink peonies or rosy pyrethrums or near a drift of yellow iris.

Anchusa has but one fault. In full flower, the top-heavy stems tend to topple, smothering nearby plants and generally creating confusion in a border. The remedy is to hammer two or three slender stakes — 1-by-2-inch lumber works well — around each clump and to

Yellow Lupine (in fruit)

wind the stakes round with strong cord to help corset this brilliant but untidy plant.

Lupine
(Lupinus polyphyllus)

Bloom: June-July
Height: 3-5 feet
Color: blue, lavender, pink, red, white, yellow, bicolor
Needs: full sun to partial shade

Photographs of grand English borders at their peak of early-summer bloom often include masses of multicolored lupines. Pictures of parts of the North American wilderness show vast stretches afloat with the blue and white spikes of this legume. But before you attempt to duplicate the display at home, take heed of one expert who says, "Not all districts are suited to the cultivation of lupines, and even the magnificent modern hybrids can be capricious if conditions are not exactly to their liking." Lupines are not usually long-lived in a garden. If they linger for four years, count yourself lucky.

Once you have a sunny site, soil pH seems to be the crucial variable. Lupines do not tolerate alkaline earth well; too much sweetness, in fact, can do them in. They are said to thrive in moist, humus-rich soil that is a little on the sour side. No wonder, then, that our best crop grew in a bed that had been liberally fertilized the previous fall with a thick layer of decayed leaves, a process that no doubt lowered the pH of our sweet, sandy soil. Peat moss does the same.

One additional difficulty arises in the cultivation of lupines: the taprooted plants do not recover well from root disturbance. It is best, then, to sow the quick-sprouting seeds directly into 4-inch pots, several seeds per pot, thinning to the single strongest seedling, and to transfer the young plants to the garden before the taproot winds itself around the bottom of the pot. The Stokes seed catalogue recommends freezing seeds for two days, then wrapping them in a damp paper towel for a day before sowing. A cool germinating temperature (54 degrees F) is also called for because "higher temperatures will actually prevent sprouting." Another tactic is to sow seeds directly into the prepared earth of a flower bed, three or four seeds in a group, 18 inches

59

between groups. Again, thin to one plant per station.

Veronica
(*Veronica* spp)

Bloom: June-August
Height: 18 inches
Color: blue
Needs: full sun

Veronica can be confusing simply because the genus contains so many garden-worthy species that vary a good deal in height, habit of growth and flowering time. Currently, our garden grows at least six species and as many named varieties, ranging from half an inch to 4 feet tall and coloring in sequence from late May until August. Three belong to June.

Veronica repens hugs the ground closely as it creeps outward to form flat mats of minute, shiny leaves sprinkled in season with small pale blue flowers. This one is safe only among scaled-down alpine plants or wedged between paving stones where foot traffic is light. Some shade is best.

More at home along a border edge or in a rock garden is the elegant *Veronica incana*, whose tufts of elliptical silver leaves, presentable year-round, provide a setting for the slim 8-inch spikes of many small amethyst florets.

Perhaps better still, due to the clarity of its blue, is *Veronica teucrium* (*V. latifolia*) in cultivars such as 'Shirley Blue' and 'Crater Lake.' If they stood upright, they would reach 18 inches, but the lax, wiry stems tend to tumble; twiggy branches pushed into the earth around the clumps keep them from sprawling on the ground. Noninvasive and hardy, this species has proven easy to cultivate in the fertile sandy loam of a sunny flower border. Nothing could be finer adjacent to pinks or coral bells than little rounded clouds of blue veronica. Aside from a bit of propping, maintenance means only trimming away the spent flower spikes in July, after which the plants revert to neat green mounds. In one season, and for many thereafter, three plants set a foot apart—crocus corms tucked between them flower while veronica is in its first stages of spring growth—create a solid path of blue for a few weeks in early summer. The brief flowering may be a drawback for some gardeners, but any lover of blue flowers cannot help appreciating their jewel-like color.

Yellow Loosestrife
(*Lysimachia punctata*)

Bloom: June-July
Height: 2½-3 feet
Color: yellow
Needs: partial shade to full sun

Yellow flowers are not plentiful in June—and just as well; this gardener is content to revel in rosiness and enjoy the subtle harmony of blue, lavender and white flowers with silver foliage. Thriving in any decent soil in sun or light shade (but with a preference for moist ground and partial shade), this tall sibling of the prostrate, wide-ranging creeping Jenny (*Lysimachia nummularia*) is a tough, care-free perennial that needs no staking or watering.

Coral Bells
(*Heuchera* spp)

Bloom: May-July
Height: 18 inches

Color: pink
Needs: full sun to partial shade

Coral bells add a touch of lightness to the front of flower beds and more rose color to June and beyond. A strong contender for Best Edging of the Summer, this plant would earn garden space even if it never flowered, on account of its decorative dark green foliage marbled and zoned with white or bronze. But flower it does. For almost two months, the lovely leaves provide a setting for a generous crop of sparkling small bells that are a favorite of hummingbirds. A single plant is nice enough, but a drift of five or more, each a foot apart from the next, makes a more effective sweep of misty color in sun or partial shade.

Coral bells bloom better if divided every three years or whenever diminished flowering tells you they are overcrowded.

Geum

(Geum quellyon)

Bloom: May-June
Height: 2 feet
Color: yellow, red

Needs: full sun

Northern gardeners have a distinct advantage when it comes to growing perennials, many of which thrive better in cooler locales than in areas where summers are excessively hot. Such is the case with geums, pretty perennials belonging to the vast family Rosaceae, which includes such diverse plants as apple trees, strawberries, spirea and, of course, roses.

Geums present no real difficulty. Like many perennials, they require humusy garden loam that drains well but holds a steady reserve of moisture. Light shade is fine in hot gardens, full sun in cooler sites. An indoor spring start from seed is recommended—soil temperature hovering around 70 degrees F for three weeks or so—for flowers the next summer.

Ornamental Onions

(Allium spp)

Bloom: May-June
Height: 3 feet
Color: lavender
Needs: full sun

Yellow Loosestrife

My favorite flowering onion, *Allium aflatunense*, is a contemporary of perennial cornflowers, and the two planted together make a close harmony of purple and blue. Early in June, stiff leafless stems lengthen to 3 feet, each supporting a tight round package of flowers-to-be wrapped in a papery husk that splits to free the unfolding buds. Soon stems are swaying with the weight of perfect 5-inch globes composed of many small lavender stars all shooting out from a central point on thread-fine stems. Once flowers fade, pods rattling with black seeds take their place, unless the seed heads are cut for dried bouquets.

Blue False Indigo
(*Baptisia australis*)

Bloom: June
Height: 4 feet
Color: blue
Needs: partial shade to full sun, lime-free soil

For nine years now, a single 4-foot baptisia plant has sat comfortably in a sunny border in our garden where it adds multiple 10-inch spikes of lavender pea-shaped flowers to June's rosiness. The nicely rounded bush of pale grey-green alfalfa-like leaves stays in good condition the season through and provides a pleasant screen for tall, possibly shabby delphiniums or hollyhocks behind it. If only baptisia flowers were true blue, red or pink, this easy plant would probably live in more gardens. It seems to thrive in almost any soil, in sun or light shade.

Foxtail Lily
(*Eremurus* spp)

Bloom: June
Height: 6 feet
Color: white, yellow, pink
Needs: full sun

Few of our perennials are as astonishing in full flower as the towering spires of eremurus, the upper third of their 6-foot leafless stems crowded with hundreds of small stars—white, yellow or rose, depending on the species.

In the home garden, they must be sited in fullest sun well away from shadowing neighbors and planted in earth that drains water like the proverbial sieve. Sandy ground is almost a must, but a light loam is possible with crumbly cow manure or compost added to nourish these robust giants. Fall is the time to plant foxtail lily roots. Take care not to bend the easily broken roots but to set them as received in an ample hole so that the crowns, or eyes—little nubs like asparagus tips at the hub of the roots—are 3 inches below ground. If there is any doubt about drainage, an inch or so of sand above and below the roots is a help. With luck, their numbers will increase slowly every spring thereafter. Once planted, they should never be moved.

Soapwort
(*Saponaria ocymoides*)

Bloom: May-June
Height: 4 inches
Color: pink
Needs: full sun

Once, in distant, simpler days, a washing powder was made of soapwort, a European perennial whose roots yield, according to one source, "a suds-producing substance particularly effective for dissolving fat, grease and resins." The same sudsy roots have been used to produce a head on beer. Today, this 10-inch plant is a showy June edger or rock garden dweller that foams with five-petaled pink flowers above a tangle of wiry stems clothed in small oval leaves.

Easy to raise from either seed or starter plants, mounds of soapwort widen eventually to fill a square foot or more of space. A shearing, as for pinks, keeps soapwort thrifty and dense.

Gas Plant
(*Dictamnus fraxinella*)

Bloom: June
Height: 2½ feet
Color: white
Needs: full sun

Here is a perennial that, like a peony, can live in a garden for decades without lifting, dividing or other kindly meddling on a gardener's part, provided it is set in deep, fertile earth at the start and given its own yard-wide circle of space in a sunny or partially shaded flower

bed. Foliage, dark green and leathery, stays fresh from spring till fall and makes an attractive setting for the foot-long, tapered spires of florets, either white or rosy purple, that decorate the plant in June.

By some accounts, the flowers give off such a quantity of fragrant, volatile oils on a sultry summer night that if a lighted match is held to one, a little puff of flame will shoot out from the flower's mouth—hence the common name.

Perennial Salvia
(*Salvia superba*)

Bloom: June-August
Height: 18 inches
Color: blue
Needs: full sun

Flower borders need the shadowy effect of deep dusky colors among the light yellows and rosy pinks. Few perennials glow as darkly brilliant as a mass planting of *Salvia superba*, a 2½-foot-tall, self-supporting, drought-resistant, bug-proof and long-flowering relative of cooking sage. It returns year after year, with no designs on more gar-

Soapwort

den space. Each June, its aromatic gray-green foliage is topped by a thick crop of purple-violet flower spikes that remain colorful while iris and poppies come and go. Once in the garden, it is easy to increase into three- or four-shoot divisions in spring or fall. A good thing, too, because purple sage is that much more effective in a group of three or more.

Silver-Dollar Plant
(*Lunaria biennis*)

Bloom: June
Height: 3 feet
Color: purple and white
Needs: partial shade

Most folks know lunaria's brittle branching stems hung with round, parchmentlike seedpods as dust-gathering dried material for winter bouquets. I wonder how many gardeners would buy these "silver dollars" if they knew how easy they are to grow. In fact, this seed-scattering biennial, also called money plant and pennies-from-heaven, can soon become one of a gardener's self-inflicted weeds. If you can handle the in-

crease, money plant grows quickly from spring-sown seeds, flowers a full year after and then disappears from that spot only to spring up elsewhere. Any soil short of soggy in any site will do.

Snow-in-Summer
(*Cerastium tomentosum*)

Bloom: June
Height: 6 inches
Color: white
Needs: full sun

Another inveterate spreader, but this time underground, gray-leaved cerastium insinuates its twitchlike runners into the affairs of neighboring plants or weaves its way down a rock garden slope. While it is useful for low-maintenance plantings—a good ground cover in sun, for instance—it must always be kept well away from smaller things. We grow cerastium along the edge of a flower border and pounce with the trowel if it gets out of bounds. Its gray-white foliage is effective from spring to fall, and the crop of fluffy white blooms, truly like a little drift of snow in summer, adds to June's bounty. Seeds or

starter plants grow in any dryish soil in sun.

Peonies
(*Paeonia* spp)

Bloom: May-June
Height: 2-4 feet
Color: pink, red, white
Needs: full sun

When the peonies flower, Larkwhistle reaches one of its high points, a celebration of the coming of summer with a spectacular burst of crimson, pink and white. I always wonder how such opulent blooms can grow from such sturdy, no-nonsense plants; hardy far into the north, they are almost invariably vigorous and healthy and are capable of keeping their corners of the garden full and fresh six months a year and of standing their ground for decades when left to their own wild ways.

The surest way to extend peony times is to plant early, midseason and late-blooming cultivars. At Larkwhistle, peonies span five weeks or more, from the end of May until about mid-July.

Rain or shine, double peonies are sure

Open the world of HARROWSMITH to a special friend or family member with a Gift Subscription. HARROWSMITH is a gift that will be read, reread and discussed for the entire year. Pay just $15, saving $9 off the basic subscription price. If the attached card has been taken, write:

THE CREAMERY
CHARLOTTE, VT 05445

Share the Wealth

... and save $9

~~$24~~ *$15*

YES. I'd like to share HARROWSMITH with a friend or relative.

Your Name: _____

Address_____

City _____ State ____ Zip _____

Gift Name:_____

Address_____

City _____ State ____ Zip _____

☐ **Bill me**
☐ **Payment enclosed**

☐ **Start or extend my own subscription**

HARROWSMITH's basic subscription price is $24 per year. Published bi-monthly. For addresses outside the U.S., add $6 per year.

271P

to be the first flowers to fall over. After watching our peonies trail sodden blossoms on the lawn for several seasons, we decided that the few minutes it takes to support them is time well spent in view of the splendid effect. To that end, we now hammer three lengths of 1-by-2-inch lumber around each peony, close enough that the wood is partially hidden by leaves but not so close as to damage the peony crowns. We then wind three levels of sturdy string from stake to stake, making sure that the top string comes to within 8 inches or so of the flower buds—I say "buds" because staking is done before the flowers open. See that the cord is not so tight that it keeps the bush from assuming a relaxed natural shape.

Not all peonies need staking, however. Gardeners who know only the heavy doubles will find nice surprises in the single peonies (poppylike with a row of petals cupped around conspicuous central stamens) and the semi-doubles (with several overlapping rows of petals).

Given their longevity, peonies deserve thoughtful siting and careful planting in earth that will nourish them for many years; they prefer to sink their

roots into what has been described as "fat, greasy loam," a rather heavy soil well supplied with organic matter. We order the roots in summer for dormant delivery in fall; mid-September to mid-October is peony planting time. For each root, we dig an oversized hole, 2 feet or more across and 18 inches deep, piling the topsoil to one side, but hauling subsoil away. The excavation is backfilled with a mixture of about two-thirds topsoil—sometimes we borrow a wheelbarrow load of our best loam from the vegetable plot—and one-third very old, black cow manure, avoiding anything approaching fresh. Three or four shovelsful of peat moss, a shovel of wood ashes and a few trowels of bone meal are all thoroughly stirred into the blend.

Planting depth is critical. Set too deeply, peonies may never bloom. If you have a clump that has been in place and flowerless for two years or more, consider lifting it in fall, cutting the roots gingerly into three-to-five-eye sections—larger clumps may not recover for several years—and replanting the divisions at the right depth. The hard-and-fast rule is to place a measured 1½ to 2 inches of earth over the

Double White Peony

65

topmost buds – little reddish nodules that will be next year's shoots. In preparation for peonies, we trowel out enough of the prepared soil to accommodate the root at the required depth and, with the root in place, gradually fill in and firm the soil around it – fingers are the tools for this – until it is secure. A half-bucket of water settles the works.

Once established, peonies seem to thrive on benign neglect and should be left in peace. Water seems to be even more necessary for peonies than surface fertility. Although the plant itself will endure drought, its buds need moisture to mature and open. If an early dry spell hits, a few deep drinks could mean the difference between a full crop of flowers and a meager show. Late-summer moisture, too, ensures that activity continues underground in the cause of next season's bloom. Also in aid of next season, late mulching may be a good idea. Peonies remain hardy to at least minus 20 degrees F.

As landscaping tools, peonies are more versatile than most perennials. In addition to spectacular blooms, the symmetrical yard-high growth of elegant, long-lasting leaves makes the plants naturals for focal points or massed display. At Larkwhistle, peonies are a stable, persistent presence in beds and borders among more flighty or floppy perennials. Where they are grown in groups, they should be planted 3 feet apart, and the same distance should be left between peonies and other robust perennials in a mixed border.

If I could grow only one perennial, this would be it.

Dog-Day Stalwarts

Lilies and more for the midsummer garden

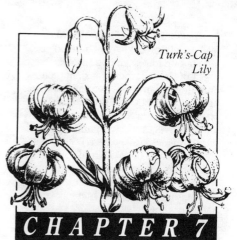

Turk's-Cap Lily

CHAPTER 7

Years ago at Larkwhistle, May and June's exuberant flowering gave way to a subdued and rather shabby midsummer garden. To say that the flower borders lapsed into green after the last peony had faded would be a polite way to describe the patchy plots of none-too-interesting foliage separated by gaps of bare earth where spring bulbs and Oriental poppies had flowered and then gone underground. With three months of decent growing weather still to come, July

67

seemed too soon for an anticlimax.

Annual flowers, we discovered, are one option for extending the color, since most of these garden transients come into flower fairly late and then carry on until frost or beyond. But annuals were at odds with our aim to grow a garden of hardy, relatively permanent perennials that would follow each other in successive waves of color from spring till fall, plants chosen and arranged with a view to masking the inevitable gaps with either persistently fine foliage or later flowers.

Clearly, we had some homework to do if we wanted to avoid the midsummer doldrums. We checked back into our favorite garden books and poked around in other gardens to see what was happening in July and August. Over several seasons, we expanded our repertoire of hardy plants to include a greater complement of late-bloomers. Once new plants—scrounged, seed-grown or mail-ordered—were at hand, we began the process of shifting things about so that perennials that were at their best at different times alternated with one another throughout a border. Sometimes we would completely replace, say, a clump of irises or a group of sweet Williams with later-blooming lythrums or daylilies. More often, we would reduce the scope of early plants to make room for hardy geraniums, scarlet bergamot or balloon flowers. Wherever there were a few square feet of empty border space, in went a clutch of lily bulbs, often with the likes of flax or violas planted over their heads for a cooling ground cover and extended bloom. Dwarf early perennials that continued to flower into July and beyond— violas and coral bells come to mind— were given places of prominence along the fronts of borders.

Becoming acquainted with the many fine perennials that bloom in midsummer was the surest way of all, we found, to keep a garden fresh and flowery after June's opulence.

Lilies
(*Lilium* spp)

Bloom: June-August
Height: 2-6 feet
Color: every color
Needs: full sun to partial shade

As the seasons turn, each phase in a bed of hardy flowers has its primary perennials around which garden pictures are composed. In April, daffodils star; in May, tulips; in June, irises, with poppies and peonies sharing top billing in some gardens. At Larkwhistle, July sees lilies in all their exotic forms and stunning colors, blooming in the company of sky blue delphiniums, misty baby's-breath, fragrant scarlet bergamot and dependable daylilies. The garden that grows a crop of lilies cannot help making the transition from June's abundance to midsummer in the most beautiful way.

In the last few years, lilies have become something of a passion with us. Besides including them in all of the flower beds, each fall we fill a 4-by-25-foot vegetable garden bed with several hundred bulbs, many of them offshoots from crowded older clumps, which we then sell to garden visitors the following October.

More than most perennials, lilies vary among themselves in flower form, the four types being: down-facing lilies, out-facing lilies, up-facing lilies and trumpet lilies.

The fact that lilies bloom in various sizes and conformations and in a color range rivaled only by iris makes them equally amenable to harmonious associations with other plants. As with tulips and iris, the possibilities for lily-based pictures are limited only by imagination, preference and the scope of a gardener's plot of land. Like most other hardy bulbs, lilies are generally planted in fall, but I have also had good luck with peat-packed lily bulbs bought from local nurseries in spring. If I see shoots pushing at the confining plastic bag and fresh roots among the moss, I reckon that the bulbs are lively and raring to grow.

With bulbs ranging from $2 apiece to $35 for 12, most of us will want to see that they live in suitable soil. Decent loam well supplied with organic matter is the medium for lilies, while heavy, excessively damp, dry or very sandy soils are to be avoided—or improved. Heavy clay needs an admixture of gritty sand or even crushed stone to lighten it and improve drainage. Since most lilies respond to a soil pH of neutral to slightly acidic, lime is usually not called for.

To plant lilies, trowel out an oversized hole to accommodate the roots without cramping, and see that soil—again, fattened with organic matter if it is your basic garden-variety earth— is

gently firmed all around the bulbs to avoid root-drying air pockets.

Most lilies sprout roots not only from the bottom of the bulbs but also from the underground portion of their stems. These "stem-rooters" are planted with 3 or 4 inches of earth over the tops of the bulbs to give stem roots somewhere to go. As with other bulbs, be guided in depth of planting by their size, with larger ones going relatively deeper. Some lily bulbs grow to softball size, notably those of tiger lilies, plants scorned by some but still among my favorites for August pictures with blue and white aconites. An exception to the rule of deep planting for large bulbs is the classically lovely white Madonna lily (*Lilium candidum*), which must be planted in August or early September with a scant inch of earth over the bulbs. This species produces a fall growth of leaves. If Madonna lilies thrive for you, let them be and resist the urge to dig them up and divide them.

Conventional garden wisdom has it that lilies like their roots in the shade and their heads in the sun—that is to say, they prefer cool moist soil to hot sun-baked sites. Clearly, a mulch is in order, either living or inert. Dwarf,

White Lily

69

Broad-Leaved Larkspur

shallow-rooted plants such as violas, flax or Carpathian harebells set among the lilies help to shade the ground, or a mulch of straw or compost can be laid down. Lilies will adapt to flickering sun or shade for half a day but flourish in sun in our relatively cool garden. Any planted in even a modicum of shade tend to lean out toward the light and are in danger of toppling when the stems are laden with flowers.

Sooner or later, a single lily bulb will grow to be a cluster. One bulb becomes two in a season, two become four and so on. When you see a plethora of leafy stems but a dearth of flowers above ground, you will know that the bulbs have increased to the overcrowded stage below. The time has come, once foliage has ripened to brown and yellow in fall, to lift a clump. Pry up the works delicately with a spading fork, being careful not to aim too close or you'll shish kebab some bulbs on the fork tines. What you will find is an aggregate of tightly packed bulbs, as well as a handful of pea-sized bulblets. If your garden is full, you'll have an embarrassment of riches to deal with, because each bulblet, like any onion set, is potentially a big flowering bulb in one

season. Unless you plan to sell lily bulbs—at several dollars apiece, among the more profitable home-garden cash crops—you'd better compost or give away the bulblets and concentrate on the big ones. After snipping off the current stems close to the bulbs, ease bulbs apart carefully by hand. If the roots are long and unwieldy, shorten them a little. Replant bulbs right away—if they must stay out of the ground for a while, damp peat moss is the storage medium, a cool shed or garage the place—in earth that has been heartened once more with humus. If, during the summer, you had noticed signs of botrytis infection, such as spotty leaves that die back exceptionally early, consider a shake-'n'-plant solution of garden sulphur in a plastic bag, in which bulbs are gently tossed before being planted.

Delphiniums
(*Delphinium* spp)

Bloom: June-July
Height: 3-6 feet
Color: blue, white, purple
Needs: full sun to partial shade, slightly alkaline soil

Surely any gardener who has seen well-grown clumps of delphiniums standing tall and stately, their reaching spires mirroring the blue of the summer sky, must yearn to grow them. The fact that they are not to be won with the mere scattering of a few seeds in any out-of-the-way corner makes them all the more enticing.

We have had good success with this showy perennial by paying attention to its few reasonable requirements.

Delphiniums take to full sun, especially in cool northern gardens, but I have seen them bloom beautifully in a foundation bed along an east-facing house wall where they caught the morning sun only. In hot gardens, some afternoon shade is a comfort, provided it is not cast by large trees close enough to steal moisture and soil nutrients. More important than site, however, is soil. Bulky, sappy perennials, delphiniums must sink their roots into deep, moist loam. I prepare a spot for lily bulbs by digging out a deep hole, removing subsoil and backfilling with topsoil and humus to give a single delphinium full-course fertility. Well-rotted cow manure is especially recommended, and a sprinkling of wood ashes is said to heighten color intensity. Drainage must be reasonably good, and a surface mulch of manure or compost, laid down anytime, can only help.

Lanky 6-foot delphiniums must have some support, or they will be on the ground after the first windstorm. We make an inconspicuous truss by hammering three pieces of 1-by-2-inch lumber (or strong, straight branches, old rake handles or what have you), each 5 feet tall, firmly into the ground around the outside of a clump. Then as the stems lengthen, we wind stout cord from stake to stake and tie the plant in at several ascending levels, but not so tightly as to give it a Scarlet O'Hara waist. Support is the goal, not strangulation.

One writer's comment about spring bulbs – "Their last state is not as lovely as their first" – applies equally to delphiniums. By the time the flowers have faded to ashen tints, the foliage is usually wind-ripped and mildewed. This is the time to cut clumps back close to ground level. With decent soil and extended growing weather, there may be a second show of flowers in October.

Delphiniums, especially the modern hybrids, cannot be counted on to stay for many years. After three or four seasons, one needs to give some thought to replacing clumps that may be deteriorating. Since they do not divide particularly well, it is back to the seed catalogues or off to a nursery for starter plants.

Bergamot
(*Monarda didyma*)

Bloom: July-August
Height: 3 feet
Color: red, pink, white, violet
Needs: partial shade to full sun

Fertile earth and moisture, too, are needed for *Monarda didyma*, a perennial of many names – bergamot, bee balm, Oswego tea. The whole plant smells deliciously of citrus and spice, and the leaves add a unique bouquet (similar to the flowery essence of Earl Grey tea) to a homemade herbal brew. A member of the mint family, bergamot is a first-rate plant for midsummer color as well. Atop 3-to-4-foot stems, the crowns of tubular flowers, sometimes one whorl above another, are always alive with the aerial acrobatics of hummingbirds.

Bergamot blooms gloriously for

weeks in July and early August for us. Give it humus-rich earth that does not dry out, or it will lose its lower leaves and never attain its full height. Give it plenty of room and a site where breezes blow freely, or it will grow lanky and mildewed. And finally, divide clumps often, first thing in spring or early in fall, or they will spread, mintlike, into a tangled mat of weak shoots.

Baby's-Breath
(*Gypsophila paniculata*)

Bloom: June-August
Height: 3 feet
Color: white, pink
Needs: full sun, alkaline soil

Everyone who has ever given or received a gift of cut flowers knows baby's-breath as that delicate, tiny-flowered filler that enhances a bouquet of showier things. But if our visitors' reactions are typical, few are aware that baby's-breath is an easily cultivated hardy perennial that can do the same in a flower bed. I can think of few places where a mist of baby's-breath would be amiss. Growing to 3 feet tall and as wide across, clouds of countless pearly blooms threaded on a weblike framework of thin, wiry stems hover lightly in a border in front of stout clumps of delphiniums and rose loosestrife or among heavy-headed daylilies, bright-colored lilies and bergamot—to name a few of gypsophila's contemporaries. Gypsophila has not just a preference but a definite need for sweet earth. Other requirements are an open sunny site and soil that drains swiftly. Drought does not menace baby's-breath, but standing water is fatal. If your garden qualifies, give some thought to the plant's initial placement, because once its anchoring taproot has burrowed deeply, you will not shift gypsophila without doing it serious damage.

Although I have raised gypsophila from seed, I do not recommend this method. Chances are, you will end up with single-flowered baby's-breath, ethereal to the vanishing point. A clutch of daffodils can be planted around gypsophila (but not too close) for early color. The bulbs do not interfere with its growth, and in no time, baby's-breath will draw a beaded curtain over the fading bulb leaves.

If it takes to your garden, gypsophila returns every year with little attention, taking several seasons to fill out to full potential. As it grows, however, a clump should be supported with two or three yard-tall stakes pounded a foot into the ground and wound around with strong string.

Monkshood
(*Aconitum* spp)

Bloom: July-August
Height: 3-4 feet
Color: blue
Needs: partial shade to full sun

Several monkshoods, members of the family Ranunculaceae and therefore related, surprisingly enough, to common field buttercups, are fine companions to the loosestrife, thriving in the same moist soil and light shade and not unlike them in height and habit. But a caution: all parts of all aconites are extremely poisonous.

Monkshoods provide pleasing color for the back of a border. Although all aconites grow slowly from seed, a clump pried from the ground in spring with a spading fork practically falls

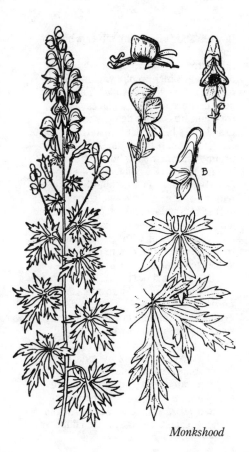

Monkshood

apart into separate divisions. Stems end in little knobby tubers that can be further eased apart by hand. Divisions establish readily in a new location. Well-enriched, moisture-holding earth supports this thirsty perennial best, in sun or partial shade. If starved, overcrowded or dry at the roots, aconites lose their lower leaves and grow stunted and yellowish. Although a mulch is a help, it is no substitute for humusy soil from the start.

Astilbe
(*Astilbe* spp)

Bloom: June-September
Height: 18 inches-3 feet
Color: lavender, pink, red, blue, white
Needs: full sun

Plants that live in moist shade seem to deal in especially lovely leaves. Ferns, hostas, Solomon's seal and sweet woodruff come to mind. Astilbes, too, fan out lush, fresh-looking greenery, in this case, compound pointed leaves sharply toothed along their edges. In some cultivars, both leaves and stems look as if they have been washed with a watercolor brush dipped in crimson, like the plumage of some exotic bird.

Most astilbe cultivars grow from 18 to 24 inches tall, but some top 3 feet. While the tallest astilbes are conspicuous accents when planted singly, the rest are more effective in groups of three or more, the plants spaced 18 inches apart. Given that one plant fattens into a multicolored clump in a year or two, it is easy enough to work up a stock of this elegant perennial by spring division. Otherwise, however, they can be left in place for many years.

Although shade is usually suggested for astilbes, at Larkwhistle they grow in full sun in an 18-inch-deep bed of loam, manure and peat moss—lime is not on their diet. Since our astilbe bed borders a concrete lily pool, it is no hardship to empty a bucket of water over the astilbes from time to time. Moisture and soil fertility are essential for this plant, especially if shade is lacking.

Yarrow
(*Achillea* spp)

Bloom: June-August

73

Yarrow

Height: 8 inches-4 feet
Color: yellow, white, red
Needs: full sun

Better in sun is the genus *Achillea*, which is high on my list of decorative, easy-care perennials, although some of the invasive sorts such as the 'Cerise Queen' cultivar of the common roadside yarrow, *A. millefolium*, and *Achillea* 'The Pearl' are best left out of small gardens. Several bring both silver and gold to the garden. Big brother of the clan is *A. filipendulina*, better known for its cultivars 'Coronation Gold,' 'Parker's Variety' and 'Gold Plate.' These 4-foot plants are ornamental from tip to toe, from the time the elegant aromatic foliage, like silver fern fronds, emerges in spring until the last of many flat heads of yellow have mellowed to autumnal brown. The taller yarrows are mid-border plants—given their bulk, one may be enough—where they shine effectively with *Salvia superba* or Shasta daisies.

Although 'Gold Plate' is a strong contender, my favorite yarrow is 'Moonshine,' a 2-foot garden-bred achillea that has traded the burnished tansy gold of the genus for clear, lemon yellow flowers above finely cut silver-white foliage.

Shorter and just right for edging or rockery is 8-inch woolly yarrow (*Achillea tomentosa* or *A. t. aurea*). This hardy little creeper from high places in Europe and Russia has densely furred, gray leaves below flat, mustard-yellow flower heads. It thrives in dry, gravelly ground but must have full sun for health. A mat of woolly yarrow is composed of many separate plantlets, each with its own roots, the whole strung together by shallow underground stems. To propagate it, you can easily detach individual crowns with clippers and trowel, or an entire mat may be lifted and eased apart.

After a season or two, a single starter plant can be conjured into a dozen to border a bed or carpet a patch of ground. For another crop of color in the same place, I push tiny bulbs of wild crocuses through the mat.

With the exception of hybrids such as 'Moonshine,' which must be purchased or propagated asexually, yarrows are easily grown from seed sown indoors or out in spring. Set seedlings in their permanent place when they are a couple of inches high.

Midsummer Daisies

Bloom: June-August
Height: 1-2 feet
Color: white, yellow
Needs: full sun

Although daisies bloom every month of the growing season save the earliest, July and August are their months to shine.

Larger versions of the ubiquitous roadside wildflowers, Shasta daisies (*Chrysanthemum maximum*) grow dark green, tongue-shaped foliage in basal clumps, from which flower stems rise from 1 to 3 feet, depending on the cultivar. Three or four plants set about 15 inches apart in decent earth – Shastas are sensitive to dryness – highlight a stretch of blue delphiniums or red bergamot with classic white flowers in a border.

Shasta daisies have one fault: they are not as hardy or as enduring as other perennials, and a severe or soggy winter of freeze and thaw is apt to kill them. Because older clumps are more vulnerable, many gardeners make a point of splitting shastas every other spring or so. Nothing could be easier, since clumps tend to fall into distinct rooted divisions as you lift them. Toss out the woody centers, and replant three-crowned chunks, firmly and slightly deeper than they were growing, in freshly fertilized soil.

A little earlier than Shastas come golden marguerites, *Anthemis tinctoria*, 2-foot lacy mounds of aromatic greenery covered with 2-inch intense yellow daisies. Quick and easy from seed at the start – a March sowing indoors will yield flowers that summer – anthemis seedlings pop up here and there in the garden ever after. Just as well, because this chamomile relative seldom lives more than three seasons. On dryish sunny banks where grass grows with difficulty, golden marguerites can be left to seed and reseed as a tallish ground cover.

Coreopsis (*Coreopsis* spp), rough-and-tumble yellow-flowered perennials, which can provide similar ground cover, are still better suited, I find, to naturalizing in hot, half-wild places than grouping in borders. Although some experts say that coreopsis endures for years, clumps in our garden crushed under snow all winter sometimes melt to a mess of soggy leaves by spring, never to rise again. Consequently, I do not count on this one for consistent color but relegate it to out-of-the-way sunny corners where it can seed at will.

Bellflowers

(*Campanula* spp)

Bloom: June-August
Height: 4 inches-3 feet
Color: blue, purple
Needs: full sun to partial shade

Campanulas may be ground-hugging dwarfs or the garden's tallest herbaceous plants. Although their flowers, always some variation on the simple bell shape, are not large or opulent, they generally come in such quantity as to make a solid splash of color, typically, soft lavender-blue or white.

Both *Campanula garganica* and *C. muralis* – the latter is sometimes smothered under the alias *C. portenschlagiana* – belong to safe nooks in a rock garden or elsewhere among small unthreatening plants. *Garganica*, all of 4 inches tall, is a little galaxy of starry blue flowers over a foot-wide mat of tiny tri-

angular leaves. *Muralis*, meaning "of the wall," looks best threading its stringy shoots along the crevices of a dry-built stone wall, where its pendant, glossy purple bells can swing freely. If planted on level ground, its flowers trail in the dust.

Back in the open border, Carpathian harebells (*Campanula carpatica*) are all aflutter with shallow, upturned bells, cloudy blue or white, that make an effective floor for wine-red lilies growing through them. Indispensable for front-of-the-border color in midsummer, 10-inch *carpatica* is easy to grow and wildly floriferous in decent, well-drained loam that has been mixed with organic matter. A true herbaceous perennial, it can be divided in early spring, if necessary, just as the new crop of leaves is showing above ground. Lift a clump, and cut it into wedges with a sharp knife; or, if you want one small piece to give away or to plant elsewhere, slice gingerly into a clump without lifting it and trowel out only the severed bit. 'Blue Chips' and 'White Chips' are garden-bred carpaticas, shorter than their parent at 6 inches. Another form, *C. c. turbinata*, is like *carpatica* but more compact.

Toward the middle of a border,

peach-leaved bellflowers, *Campanula persicifolia*, send up 2-foot stems crowded with flared bells, like carpaticas, only side-swinging and either china blue or white. The thin leaves stay close to the ground. This bellflower shines in partial shade or sun but flowers much longer if rooted in earth that stays nicely moist.

At 6 feet, *Campanula lactiflora*, the milky bellflower, is an imposing giant that can stand toward the back of a flower bed with delphiniums or aconites, where its myriad small, tubular blue bells, flared at the mouth and hung near the ends of branching stems, can rise behind bergamot or lilies.

Balloon Flower
(*Platycodon grandiflorum*)

Bloom: July-August
Height: 2 feet
Color: blue, white, pink
Needs: full sun to partial shade

Close kin to bellflowers, balloon flowers contribute what Vita Sackville-West calls "an effective splash of truly imperial purple . . . in the July-August

Peach-Leafed Bellflower

border," where I like to see them neighbored by lilies and baby's-breath and perhaps backed by pink rugosa roses, if space allows.

Their buds have given balloon flowers their common name. Before opening, each is a little inflated five-sided sack, "like a tiny lantern," says Sackville-West, "so tightly closed as though its seams had been stitched together, with the further charm that you can pop it like a fuchsia, if you are so childishly minded." The eventual flowers, on 2-foot stems, are five-lobed, deep lavender and veined with inky blue. There is also a white sort and a double variety with one flower nesting inside another.

Deep, moist, humusy earth grows them best, in sunshine or light shade. Not difficult to raise from seed but quicker from nursery plants, this slowpoke perennial flowers tentatively in its second year and takes a few seasons to clump up. A few twiggy branches pushed into the earth around balloon flowers keep their slender stems from falling over. A note: Since this is one of the last perennials to show through the earth in spring, it is the better part of wisdom to mark the location of each clump with a label so as not to snap the unseen shoots during rounds of spring cleaning or cultivation.

Evening Primrose
(*Oenothera* spp)

Bloom: June-August
Height: 10-18 inches
Color: yellow
Needs: full sun

The genus *Oenothera* consists of about 80 species native to North and South America. In spite of their common name, they are not primroses at all, but many do bloom in the evening. Others, called sundrops, bloom by day.

Here and there along our border edges, the Missouri primrose (*Oenothera missourensis*) trails over a shoulder of limestone. Lax 8-inch stems end in a cluster of longish, red-spotted green buds that open successively into showy, round, clear yellow flowers which are a full 4 inches across. If only the flowers lasted more than a day each and the plants were more compact, the Missouri primrose would be one of the better midsummer edgers. As it is, I like it as an interesting incident next to a drift of Carpathian harebells or dianthus.

Most decorative of all is *Oenothera fruticosa*, a 2½-foot evening primrose generous with its crop of cupped yellow blooms above attractive green leaves marked with maroon. A no-care mid-border perennial, *fruticosa* clumps quickly into a weed-suppressing mat of closely packed rosettes that can be divided in spring or fall. Chances are, however, that you will need to curb this mover rather than increase it. I have seen *fruticosa* used both as a tallish ground cover and as a herbaceous hedge. In a flower bed, it combines well with scarlet Maltese cross and daylilies of any hue. Easily cultivated, all evening primroses crave sun and warm ground but do not need much in the way of fertile soil. Seed will grow them, but starter plants are a shortcut to first-season flowers.

Maltese Cross
(*Lychnis chalcedonica*)

Bloom: June-July
Height: 2½ feet
Color: red

Needs: full sun

Lychnis means lamp in Greek, a name that suits the flaming flowers of *Lychnis chalcedonica*. Native to northern Russia and Siberia, this decorative perennial—a natural with tall evening primroses, if you like the hot contrast of red and yellow—tops 2½-foot stems of pleasant greenery with flat heads of clustered, vivid scarlet flowers, their four petals arranged in the shape of a Maltese cross. Flourishing in any fertile soil, this brilliant thing is completely hardy and loves the sun. It is noninvasive and can be left to grow in peace as long as it is doing well. If an older clump begins to wane, there will likely be replacement seedlings nearby.

Mullein
(*Verbascum* spp)

Bloom: June-September
Height: 3-6 feet
Color: white, yellow
Needs: full sun

Almost anyone who has traveled country roads has seen the conspicuous grey-flannel rosettes of common mullein (*Verbascum thapsus*), whose downy spires are sparsely set with five-lobed yellow blossoms. If this species is a trifle weedy for flower beds—I do know one gardener who lets a few interloping rosettes stay if they are not in the way—two European species are among the most striking plants of midsummer. Like other mulleins, these suit the many common names that connect them with light: candlewick plant, hag's taper, torches and the German *konigskerze*, or king's candles.

Like a candelabrum when in full bloom, *Verbascum olympicum* is a branching Greek relative of our single-stalked native mullein. Here is a truly Olympian 6-footer to shine at the very back of a flower bed or to be naturalized in a wild garden or in the corners of a vegetable patch. The first year from seed, wide woolly rosettes develop. The next season, the spot is alight with yellow blossoms from July until September.

Left to seed, Greek mullein finds its own way around the garden. If it is needed in a specific place, seedling mulleins can be shifted when they are still fairly small. Later on, you will not get the hefty plants out of the ground

Dark Mullein

without root damage and wilting leaves.

Few plants at Larkwhistle draw as much comment or as many requests for seeds as the Turkish mullein, *Verbascum bombyciferum*. Known in one catalogue as 'Arctic Summer,' as 'Silver Spire' in another, this is a species so thickly coated with downy wool, both leaf and stalk, as to be entirely silver-white. In the dry sandy soil of a raised iris bed, Turkish mulleins grew beautifully into head-high wands studded with clear yellow flowers.

A first step with mulleins is to find the seeds. Start the pepper-fine seeds indoors, six or eight to a 4-inch pot, thinning eventually to the single sturdiest seedling. After a month or so, when the plants fill the pots, set them in the garden where they are to flower. I like to situate mulleins where their silver first-year rosettes will show to best advantage. Turkish mullein must live in full sun, but the Greek will flower in light shade if it must. Leave them to seed; even the flower stalks have an interesting outline, and the seeds are a favourite winter forage for chickadees. Mulleins will thus linger in and around the beds perennially, sharing space with the other midsummer inhabitants.

Golden Knapweed
(*Centaurea macrocephala*)

Bloom: July
Height: 4 feet
Color: yellow
Needs: full sun

Another rather unusual perennial, this hardy kin to blue annual cornflowers grows a lush clump of rough-textured, oblong leaves and shoots up strong 4-foot stems, each topped by perfectly round, light brown buds that rustle like strawflowers if you tousle them. Buds do not actually open, but rather, flowers emerge from them; first a few yellow threads poke out, and soon a fluffy golden cornflower, very attractive to butterflies, sits jauntily on top. After the flowers have faded, the little brown globes become perfect packages for maturing seeds.

Sun and fertile earth grow this bulky but self-supporting perennial best. Start with seeds or nursery plants, but once they are established, leave golden knapweed alone to clump up without division or casual shifting from place to place. Your reward will surely be a grander show each year.

Sea Holly
(*Eryngium spp*)

Bloom: July-August
Height: 2 feet
Color: blue
Needs: full sun

Sea hollies are a species of *Eryngium* that seem at times to be more mineral than vegetable. Growing to 2½ feet, *Eryngium amethystinum*'s well-branched, glinting stems, clothed in white-veined heart-shaped leaves, mature from a mercury sheen to silvery blue as an abundant crop of pseudo-flowers appears. En masse, this sea holly becomes a misty cloud, a fine setting for ruby or rose lilies or gladioli of any hue.

All eryngiums, botanically related to dill, angelica and other members of the family Umbelliferae, grow best in sandy well-drained earth that need not be overly fertile. In cold wet clay, they tend to rot away. As well, they need an open, sunny position, and once established, they should not be disturbed or divided. New plants are best raised from your own seed, collected as soon as it is ripe and sown while still fresh. Like other umbelliferous plants, sea holly seed loses its spark quickly. Probably a few baby sea hollies will appear near the mother plant, and these can be set out elsewhere if needed.

Hardy Geraniums
(*Geranium* spp)

Bloom: May-September
Height: 12-15 inches
Color: pink, blue, white, red
Needs: full sun

Geraniums are a confusing lot. The annual bedding plants most gardeners know as geraniums are more properly called pelargoniums. True perennial geraniums (also called cranesbills because of their long, beaklike seedpods) are subtle plants that are far less well known or appreciated.

Our introduction to hardy geraniums began with *Geranium sanguineum*, a useful perennial that grows into nicely rounded, foot-high mounds of elegant lobed leaves over a tangled network of

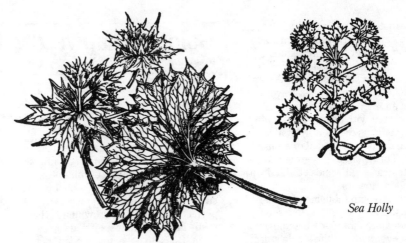

Sea Holly

wiry, reddish stems. From midsummer onward, a succession of simple round blossoms, like little magenta saucers, decorates the plants. Pretty toward the front of flower beds, this hardy geranium can also be massed as a ground cover or allowed to naturalize at will down a difficult-to-plant slope or in half-wild places. The pleasant foliage stays freshly green until fall and then colors in harmony with the autumnal scene.

Geranium endressii is like *sanguineum* in height and habit, but its flowers are pure rose pink veined with red. Bloom-

ing over a remarkably long period, this species is just right for massing as a ground cover, either in sun or partial shade, where it helps to crowd out weeds. I have noticed that *endressii*, which is said to do best in a damp climate such as that of the Pacific Northwest, wilts badly and stops flowering during a spell of drought; humus-rich earth, mulch and a few deep drinks, however, will help. The cultivar 'Wargrave Pink' is a darker rose.

At 2 feet high, *Geranium grandiflorum* is a taller species for mid-border.

80

Cupped flowers, a deep but clouded blue, are veined with maroon. Suitable for sun or light shade, this hardy Russian native and its cultivar 'Johnson's Blue' recommend themselves for low-maintenance gardens on account of their fine and lasting greenery and their generous crop of blue.

A protected corner of a rock garden or somewhere along the edge of a flower bed well away from strong-growing neighbors is the place for *Geranium* 'Ballerina,' a neat 6-inch perennial generously endowed with soft rose flowers conspicuously veined and centered with maroon. All hardy geraniums have long, ranging roots that do not divide well; small slips stolen from the outside of a clump, however, may have a few incipient roots attached, and these bits can be treated as cuttings or simply planted out and kept moist until they take.

Seed is the surest route to geranium species in the garden, although you may have to search several catalogues to find them. Thompson and Morgan is one source. But however you get them, cranesbills are easily grown, thriving in any decent garden loam in any place, in sun or partial shade.

Potentilla
(Potentilla spp)

Bloom: June-frost
Height: 1-3 feet
Color: yellow, apricot, pink, white
Needs: full sun to partial shade

Kin of geums, potentillas (or cinquefoils) are most familiar as exceedingly hardy, low (to 3 feet) shrubs. Several are native, others foreign or garden-bred. Their tangled, arching stems are set with round five-petaled flowers, which are like small single roses. Commonly yellow, they also crop up dressed in white or washed-out orange. Several shrubby cinquefoils are compact and restrained enough to mix with herbaceous plants. Especially pretty here is the 2½-foot *Potentilla fruticosa farreri*, whose soft, buttery blossoms appear in time to make a picture with creamy and deeper yellow iris behind an edging of golden thyme and a few flakes of blue flax. They continue into midsummer to accompany lilies, yarrows and the like. Golden potentillas are also useful as tall, permanent ground covers in dryish, sunny places.

Hollyhock
(Alcea rosea)

Bloom: July-September
Height: 4-9 feet
Color: pink, red, yellow, peach, purple, white
Needs: full sun

At the very back of most of our flower borders, tall swaying hollyhocks fly their colors from July onward, often into September. Flared, funnel-shaped flowers are shaded from pink to scarlet and deepest crimson, from pale yellow to apricot, peach and plum-purple.

Seeds, preferably sown outdoors where they are to flower, are the best route to hollyhocks in the garden. Even though young plants move fairly well, the earth occasionally falls away from the thonglike roots, and they are set back. Besides, seeding *in situ* saves the work of transplanting. Left to seed, hollyhocks will spring up everywhere and surprise you by flowering in colors unlike those of the parent plants.

Hollyhocks would likely be more popular if they did not succumb so easily to rust, a fungal disease whose nasty or-

81

ange spots can quickly render a clump leafless. One possible remedy is garden sulphur sprayed or dusted on the leaves. Breezes blowing freely around the plants also help keep rust at a minimum. Another solution is to plant hollyhocks at the very back of a border, where their stems will be hidden by the growth of peonies, gas plants, baptisias or aconites in front. And since young plants are apt to be healthier, we remove badly infected older clumps and leave new seedlings to carry on.

Although I have seen them flourishing in dry gravelly ground, hollyhocks respond to the rich earth of the perennial border, where they often reach 10 feet. For many years, I preferred the fat doubles but now find them graceless next to the simple singles, perhaps because of the comment that doubles look "like those toilet-paper decorations on wedding cars" – enough to put one off any flower.

Anemone

Season's
Finale

Blooming into the frosts

CHAPTER 8

With seeding, transplanting and staking accomplished and weeds more or less in check, the lazy, hazy days of August and early September bring a lull in flower garden activity before the full fall schedule of dividing perennials, rearranging parts of the garden picture, improving soil fertility, planting bulbs, cleaning up, composting and tucking the garden in for winter. For me, the first fall frost, which usually occurs here around the end of September, rings the back-to-work bell after a late-summer hiatus. The flowers in this chapter are those that colorfully carry the garden through this relatively effortless time. Some continue to bloom even after the first frost.

Phlox
(*Phlox paniculata*)

Bloom: July-August
Height: 3 feet
Color: pink, lavender, blue, red, orange, white
Needs: full sun to partial shade

Gardeners who aim to keep their flower beds showing color until fall have many late-summer perennials from which to choose, including the hardy, dependable *Phlox paniculata*, a North American native that has traded its original dim magenta for hybrid shades of pink, crimson, purple, white or scarlet.

The finest phlox I know grows unattended in the moist black earth of a neighbor's lightly shaded streamside garden. Lush and healthy after many years, the plants are decorated every August with cones of penny-round lilac flowers on 4-foot stems well furnished with dark green foliage.

Noninvasive and completely hardy into the coldest regions, phlox can be planted in spring or fall. Start with either named nursery plants or pieces from fellow gardeners. Seeds take forever, and you are never sure what color they will yield. Self-sown seedlings are also variable in color and should be removed or treated as weeds.

To divide phlox into three- or four-shoot wedges, cut down between the shoots with a strong, sharp knife and keep cutting to sever the woody roots. If a hot, dry spell hits, spring-split phlox must have plenty of water until they put out vital new roots. Some experts suggest lifting, dividing and resetting phlox in newly enriched ground every three years or so, an easy task with primroses or coral bells but a daunting one with heavyweight phlox. If plants are flowering well, I am all for laissez-faire. As an alternative to division, I sometimes thin the annually increasing shoots to 8 or 10 of the strongest in early spring and then mulch the clumps with leaves laid over compost and/or manure. Lots of water, particularly during budding and blooming, is a must.

Daylilies
(*Hemerocallis* spp)

Bloom: June-September
Height: 12 inches-4 feet
Color: all colors but white and blue
Needs: full sun to partial shade

"Beautiful for a day" is the translation of the apt Greek genus name for daylilies. But despite fleeting flowers that last only a day apiece, daylilies recommend themselves to gardeners looking for trouble-free summer color. Completely hardy and apparently immune to insects and diseases, daylilies sprout a sheaf of decorative long-lasting leaves, reed-narrow and arching, below many-hued funnel-shaped flowers that keep on coming—one after another, day by day—for weeks. If early, midseason and late-blooming sorts are planted, there will be daylilies from June until almost September.

Tough in the extreme, daylilies—either the early, soft yellow, fragrant "lemon lilies," *Hemerocallis flava*, or the robust Indian red *H. aurantiaca*—often survive in old, untended country gardens alongside faithful flag iris, wildly suckering lilacs and crowded poet's narcissus. In many locales, they have escaped the confines of gardens and decorate roadsides and ditches like any native.

Once relegated to no-account garden corners, they have recently stepped into the limelight dressed in a new array of colors—peach and pink, soft purple, bold reds and oranges and shades of yellow, copper and russet; some are zoned with a darker color or are prettily crimped along the petal edges. But for all the changes worked by hybridists, the plant retains its sturdy constitution and still adapts to sun or partial shade, hot gardens or cold and almost any soil short of dust-dry, with a definite preference for well-manured earth that retains a modicum of moisture over a dry summer. A mulch of old manure, straw, compost or leaves keeps up fertility and reduces maintenance to near zero; it is not even necessary to cut away foliage in fall. During winter, let it lie where it falls (unless you are bothered by slugs), and new shoots will push through the tangle come spring.

Perfect for the middle sections of perennial beds, daylilies associate well with later-blooming, true (that is, bulbous) lilies. The curious orange of old-fashioned tiger lilies is just right with all but purple cultivars, and wands of tall blue aconite could complete the picture nicely.

Daylilies are also at home beside a stream or pond—but not standing in water—in the company of astilbes, Siberian iris, lythrums, hostas and moisture-loving ferns. Excellent for massing as a tall, weed-smothering ground cover, they can fringe a band of shrubs or be naturalized in half-wild spaces with tall mulleins, gloriosa daisies (*Rudbeckia* spp), heliopsis and other self-sufficient plants. More formally, they stand as specimens in city gardens, along the walkway to a front door or on either side of entrance steps, where their arching, light green leaves are as decorative as the here-today-gone-tomorrow flowers. Daylily varieties abound, but I can put in a good word for 'Hyperion,' a vigorous older cultivar that is tall, lemon yellow and fragrant. Hybrid daylilies, too, are not as invasive as the old rusty species.

Although I have started them from seed, a fairly easy process that yields second-season flowers from a spring sowing, I prefer to select specific colors

Daylily

85

Helenium

of named cultivars from a nursery or catalogue to fit the picture. But division is also possible, either from one's own stock or a friend's garden. Daylilies can be split with ease in early spring, just as new shoots show through the ground. To divide: Lift a clump—much more easily said than done—and cut carefully between the shoots and down through the roots with a sharp knife. More than once, I have shifted daylilies in full flower to vacant spots in the borders, a task that requires careful digging and an extra hand or two to lift the heavy clumps into a wheelbarrow. Firm planting and lots of water ensure that the plants survive the untimely move. Except for propagation, however, division is neither necessary nor desirable; like peonies, gas plants and baby's-breath, hemerocallis improve with age and should be left alone as long as they are flowering well.

Helenium
(*Helenium autumnale*)

Bloom: August-October
Height: 3 feet
Color: yellow, red

Needs: full sun

Before I grew heleniums—the misnamed sneezeweed, or, more pleasantly, Helen's flower—I had seen them growing only once, but wonderfully well, in a friend's clay-bound, sometimes soggy garden. Raised from spring-sown seed, the strain 'Mound Mixture' (from Park Seeds) bloomed the second season, revealing abundant, 2-inch daisy flowers with ray petals flaring smartly downward from a dark central disk. I was especially taken by the color range—clear yellow, maroon, shades of orange and, nicest of all, one with petals streaked yellow and rust red, intense at first but mellowing to overall coppery hues.

Heleniums soon grow into 3- or 4-foot-tall clumps of distinct and easily detached rosettes, each with its own roots. A slip of each color from our friend's garden was our start with a perennial that provides almost six weeks of late-summer color. And this bugproof, self-supporting plant is not hard to grow in sun or very light shade, as long as its need for humusy moist earth is met. In our dry sandy garden, we plant heleniums in well-manured soil and mulch them over summer. Even so, we are prepared to soak them deeply at the first sign of wilting.

When weaker growth and fewer flowers indicate that the plants are crowded or undernourished (perhaps after four or five years), the time has come to split a clump and start over with lively three-crowned divisions. Turn more humus into the ground before setting the divisions 16 to 20 inches apart. A 6-inch layer of straw or evergreen boughs will see plants through winters that are intensely cold. First-rate perennials, heleniums deserve space in more gardens.

Hosta
(*Hosta* spp)

Bloom: July-September
Height: 1-2½ feet
Color: lavender, white
Needs: partial shade to full sun

Close kin to hemerocallis, hostas (formerly called *Funkia*) are cultivated in much the same way except that they have a decided preference for shadowy places, especially in hot, dry gardens. They sprout some of the garden's loveliest leaves—broadly heart-shaped, attractively veined and puckered, wavy-edged and colored shades of green, grey or slate blue, often streaked or banded with white or cream. In general, hosta flowers are not flamboyant, but the little lavender or white bells swinging from slender stems (up to 18 inches long) make a pleasant show where the plants are grown in generous groups. The plantain lily, *Hosta plantaginea*, with its wands of fragrant white flowers above broad lettuce-green leaves, is a likely prospect for such an assemblage, and with damp soil, it is even comfortable in the sun.

Neat and clumping in habit, hostas are formal plants for massing on 15-inch centers in conspicuous places where one wants easy, persistent cover. Or they can be set singly, as focal accents, along a walkway or at regular intervals in a shaded border. At Larkwhistle, a grand silver-leaved hosta, *Hosta sieboldiana*, grows with almost tropical luxuriance in moist, fertile earth beside a homemade water lily pool, where it softens the pool's sharp concrete edge. Wherever you place hostas, consider planting bluebells (the common *Scilla sibirica*) and snowdrops around them for a show of color weeks before the late-rising hostas unfurl.

To increase a favorite hosta, lift a well-anchored clump out of the ground with a strong shovel—I have snapped several spading forks while struggling to pry up both hostas and daylilies—and slice cleanly down between shoots and roots with a sharp knife. Wedges supplied with three or four shoots make an immediate effect, but even a single-crowned piece will expand to full size in a season or two. Like all leafy plants, hostas respond with lush, healthy growth if nitrogen-rich manure, leaf mould or compost is stirred into the ground before planting or is laid down as a top dressing—or both; it is scarcely possible to overfeed them.

Heliopsis
(*Heliopsis* spp)

Bloom: June-September
Height: 3½ feet
Color: yellow
Needs: full sun

Heliopsis, sometimes called false or orange sunflower, is another North

American native composite that, like helenium, thrives best in moist earth and full sun—a combination that can be tricky to arrange in many gardens unless one turns plenty of humus into the ground, lays down a summer mulch and turns on the hose when necessary.

A robust, almost coarse perennial, heliopsis is perhaps better suited to country gardens than to trim city spaces. It can grapple for root room with strong-growing daylilies, lythrums, Siberian irises and the like or be left to its own devices in damp, half-tamed corners, where its strong 4-foot stems, clothed top to bottom with heart-shaped leaves, support 3-inch, single or fluffy double daisies tinted sunflower-yellow. Each spring, more shoots emerge from gradually widening clumps until a plant may be 4 feet across and rather too leafy for its crop of flowers.

Heliopsis grows quickly from seed and may flower the first summer from an early start. Better than the original species, *Heliopsis scabra,* are the varieties 'Goldgreenheart,' 'Incomparabilis' and others that are less robust than their parent—an advantage in this case. All bloom for almost a month and can be left in place for many years.

Perennial Sunflowers

(*Helianthus* spp)

Bloom: August-September
Height: 6 feet
Color: yellow
Needs: full sun

Many vegetable gardens grow a stand of the tall, heavy-headed annual sunflowers *Helianthus annuus*, whose black-shelled seeds are the best of snack foods and yield a fine cooking oil as well. I hesitate, however, to recommend the less familiar perennial sunflowers, many of which are North American natives. Gangling giants that can grow out of bounds and be altogether more trouble than they are worth, they are perhaps better suited to wild or naturalistic gardens, even soggy places. Like the related heliopsis, perennial helianthus, which are always yellow, can effectively brighten forgotten corners of farm gardens, where their flopping ways above ground and the aggressive underground wandering of some species will not threaten other plants. Our own lesson came years ago, when we set a small, innocent-looking shoot of an unidentified helianthus in a perennial bed. It was only with the utmost diligence that, seasons later, we finally succeeded in extracting the last scrap of its wildly running rootstock.

But among these vegetable invaders—the prolific Jerusalem artichoke is another greedy sunflower—are more restrained species, notably *Helianthus multiflorus*. Growing about 5 feet tall, it is as compact and controlled as a sunflower gets. With its dark green foliage below many round flowers, shaded yellow to orange depending upon the cultivar, *multiflorus* makes a fine background for white phlox and lingers long enough to flower alongside lavender-colored hardy asters.

Black-Eyed Susans

(*Rudbeckia* spp)

Bloom: July-September
Height: 2-3 feet
Color: yellow
Needs: full sun

Yellow daisy-type flowers abound in

the North American wilds. In addition to a host of native sunflowers, sneezeweeds, small yellow asters, coreopsis and the weedy ranks of dandelions, sow thistles and goat's beard, there are perky black-eyed Susans (*Rudbeckia hirta*), which decorate meadows, roadsides and open woods from the Prairies to the Atlantic. Suitable for naturalizing in half-wild corners of large gardens, these self-seeding native plants bloom too sparingly to earn space in a perennial bed.

More lavish and floriferous are gloriosa daisies, big yellow hybrid rudbeckias often zoned with chocolate-brown or Indian red. Truly glorious in a mass but short-lived—virtually annuals at Larkwhistle—gloriosa daisies nevertheless often reappear year after year from their own hardy seeds. Even 'Goldilocks' and 'Marmalade,' recently developed compact cultivars said by one seed catalogue to be long-lived, seldom survive the first winter in our garden, although they cover themselves with showy yellow daisies during the first summer after early indoor seeding.

In many nearby farm gardens, golden glow, a fluffy, double-flowered sport of *Rudbeckia laciniata*, grows unattended,

but the 6-foot perennial is so lanky and weak-kneed that wind and rain always bring it down. And it's invasive to boot. Although it is useful for screening unsightly outbuildings or filling difficult corners with sprays of mustard-yellow bloom in early autumn, gardeners looking for good border plants should give golden glow a miss.

Best of the black-eyed Susans for flower beds are *Rudbeckia fulgida* and its more compact cultivar, 'Goldsturm,' 2-to-3-foot mounding plants whose nondescript greenery is all but hidden under a blanket of 3-inch yellow, dark-eyed daisies. Even a single plant makes a fine drift of color.

Autumn sun is the apt moniker for another native rudbeckia, *Rudbeckia nitida*—3 to 12 feet tall depending on soil and site—that displays a crop of lemon yellow daisies with ray petals flared down around greenish central disks. This one needs staking, but 'Goldquelle,' a double zinnia-like sport, supports its 4-foot stems without props.

Vigorous branching plants, rudbeckias need plenty of elbowroom and associate well with 'Goldplate' yarrow, white phlox, globe thistles, heliopsis and the taller ornamental grasses. Where there

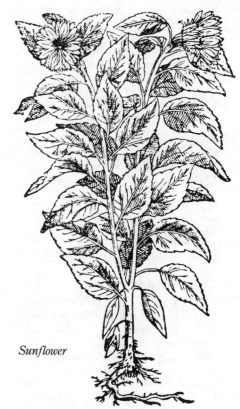

Sunflower

is space enough, 'Goldsturm' is extraordinarily effective in a garden bed adjacent to the cream and green striped grass *Miscanthus sinensis* 'Variegatus.' All rudbeckias grow quickly from seed and may yield first-summer flowers from an April sowing indoors. Most self-sow. Lots of sun and decent loam are all they need to thrive.

Sea Lavender
Statice
(*Limonium* spp)

Bloom: July-September
Height: 18 inches
Color: lavender, blue, yellow, white, red
Needs: full sun

Annual statices in all their many colors are among the most familiar dried flowers for winter bouquets. But in the late-summer flower garden, a perennial relative, *Limonium latifolium*, does what baby's-breath does in July, that is, lightens more substantial things such as phlox, coneflowers and heleniums.

From a ground-level tuft of smooth and elongated leaves, this perennial sends up branching foot-high stems set with a myriad of tiny lavender flowers—little amethyst gems when the dew collects on them. Misty and delicate in effect, these blooms dry well for winter bouquets that can also include yarrow heads, poppy seedpods, dried globe thistles and sea holly. More effective in the garden in groups of three or more, with individual plants set about 16 inches apart, sea lavender plants need only full sun and nourishing, light loam and are best set at the front of flower beds where they can be seen in their entirety.

Purple Coneflower
(*Echinacea purpurea*)

Bloom: July-September
Height: 3 feet
Color: pink, white
Needs: full sun

Botanically connected to the rudbeckias are the strange but showy purple coneflowers, whose fully expanded blossoms have narrow, gracefully twisted mauve petals that flare downward around central cones bristling with little spiked, orange-tipped seeds-in-the-making. Since the crown-shaped buds develop slowly into full-blown flowers, each lasts an exceptionally long time, a fact that compensates for their meager numbers. Here, 8 or 10 coneflowers is considered a good crop from an established clump.

Growing as tall as 4 feet, echinacea clumps seldom survive division, so it is best to leave them alone once they are settled. Started from seed indoors in spring, they yield a few flowers the first season, then return as stronger clumps with more blooms the next and the next. But then, just when you are counting on coneflowers for yet another summer, a hard winter may take the older clumps. The observant gardener will likely find young, self-sown coneflowers near the wilted parent. Look for ground-level tufts of dark green pointed leaves, deeply veined and attached to short stalks. If they are well placed, leave seedlings where they are to fatten up and flower. If not, carefully shift them to better quarters.

Like heleniums and other late-summer composites, echinacea thrives best in humus-rich (hence, moist) earth, in

Globe Thistle

full sun in cooler gardens but tucked out of the mid-day glare in hot sites.

Globe Thistles
(*Echinops ritro*)

Bloom: July-September
Height: 4-5 feet
Color: blue
Needs: full sun

Visitors to Larkwhistle find globe thistles either weird and wonderful or weedy; but whether they feel pleasure or puzzlement, most notice this strange yet striking perennial. Bright colors are not the attraction of this daisy relative but, rather, bold architectural foliage and perfectly round flower heads. Hoary gray-green leaves, indented and spiny like overgrown silver holly, arch out from stout 4-foot stems topped with steel blue, spiky spheres that change very little whether in their bud, flowering or seed phase. Cut while in bud and hung in an airy, shaded place to dry, globe thistles hold their round shape for winter bouquets.

Fine companions for phlox or heleniums, globe thistles take to any well-drained sunny site, provided their roots find enough moisture to support their robust growth. Groups of three, each plant set 2 feet from the next, form an arresting feature toward the center of an island bed behind black-eyed Susans, showy stonecrop, any of the yellow yarrows or mounds of hardy geraniums showing the last of their pink or white saucers.

Black Snakeroot
(*Cimicifuga racemosa*)

Bloom: July-August
Height: 6 feet
Color: white
Needs: partial to full shade

Fred and Mary Ann McGourty, who cultivate an astonishing 700 species and cultivars of hardy perennials at Hillside Garden in Connecticut, count black snakeroot among their top 10 selections—high praise indeed. Well grown in moist, humusy soil in sun or partial shade, snakeroot, a denizen of moist woodlands from Ontario to Georgia, is a robust but graceful 6-footer decorated for almost a month with tapered plumes

91

of pearly buds and fluffy white blooms above fanning, compound dark green foliage.

An effective and enduring element at the back of borders, snakeroot "retains a great deal of architectural character," says one writer, even after its flowers have faded. Because it is such a tall, slender thing, three plants grouped together make more impact than a single specimen. Cimicifuga is well placed behind medium-height ferns and is fine with rose loosestrife, daylilies, pink phlox or crimson astilbe.

Cimicifuga can be divided carefully or raised, albeit slowly, from fresh seeds. A better plan, however, is to set potted nursery plants a full 2 feet apart in the best soil you can manage, and leave them to clump up undisturbed.

Gooseneck Flower
(*Lysimachia clethroides*)

Bloom: July-August
Height: 3½-4 feet
Color: white
Needs: partial shade

Although the gooseneck flower has lived at Larkwhistle for only two seasons, it has already proved to be one of our finest late-summer perennials—problem-free, self-supporting and elegant in bloom. I wonder why it crops up so seldom in nurseries or gardens. It grows 3½ to 4 feet tall, its sturdy stems set with narrow, dusty green leaves, ending in gracefully drooping, elongated tapers. With its small, starry white flowers that continue to open in succession for almost a month, the gooseneck flower looks in profile like the head and neck of a swan or goose. Since faded flowers drop off cleanly, the plant appears fresh all through its flowering season.

A Japanese native and kin of the June-blooming yellow loosestrife, the gooseneck flower has clumped up very quickly in the moist, fertile earth (equal parts loam, manure and peat moss) of our "quiet garden."

Useful for mixed borders, for wild gardens that never get too dry or along the margins of streams or ponds, the gooseneck flower needs no care once it settles in. But mark the spot where it grows, because it is one of the last plants to show through the ground in spring. If you forget its location, you're apt to break off hidden shoots during early cultivation and cleanup. Spring bulbs, daffodils especially, planted around clumps of lysimachia bring early color to the same spot.

Obedient Plant
(*Physostegia virginiana*)

Bloom: August-October
Height: 3-4 feet
Color: pink, white
Needs: partial shade to full sun

An easy—a little too easy, some might say—but neglected late-summer perennial, the obedient plant (also known as false dragonhead) shoots up 4-foot, self-supporting square stems densely clothed with glossy, deep green oblong leaves that make even flowerless clumps presentable all season long. By mid-August, an abundant crop of 8-inch symmetrical spires of pretty white- or purple-lipped flowers, like small snapdragon blossoms, appear. If you have nothing else to do, you can reposition the individual flowers, which are attached to their stems by the botanical equivalent of a ball-and-socket joint;

however you turn them, left or right, up or down, the flowers stay put, a trait that has suggested the common name, obedient plant.

If only its roots were as amenable. A mint relative, physostegia has but one fault: its outward-creeping rootstock expands, mintlike, rather too quickly for the comfort of less aggressive things nearby. The plant's wandering ways need not deter you from growing it, however. Any shoots that move out of bounds can simply be sliced away and dug out. Like mint, the obedient plant thrives in moist loam, in sun or partial shade, and will run beautifully wild along the banks of a stream or pond.

Artemisia
(*Artemisia* spp)

Bloom: August-September
Height: 3-5 feet
Color: foliage-only or white
Needs: full sun

Most garden artemisias are aromatic silver-leaved herbs valued for their persistent, finely cut foliage, which serves as a soft-toned filler in beds of bright flowers. Some species are flowerless, while some send up sprawling wands of dowdy yellow-green buttons. Among the best for the northern perennial garden are:

•*Artemisia* 'Silver Mound,' whose feathery, foot-high symmetrical hummocks of thread-fine, silver-blue leaves make an excellent edging where the plants have room to spread out in full sun and perfectly drained soil;

•*Artemisia absinthium* 'Lambrook Silver,' an improved wormwood that fills a space 3 feet tall and wide with delicately incised, silver-white foliage. Pruning in spring and again in midsummer keeps this exuberant perennial shapely;

•*Artemisia abrotanum*, or southernwood, a robust, hoary-leaved 5-foot herb that shines all season long toward the back of a flower bed, where it is especially pleasing with foreground clumps of *Achillea* 'Moonshine,' *Salvia superba* and purple coneflowers. Prune as for 'Lambrook Silver';

•*Artemisia ludoviciana* 'Silver King,' a showy but extremely invasive bit of garden silverware that should be grown either where it can be contained or where there is room for its rapid

Common Wormwood

spread.;

•*Artemisia lactiflora*, an exception to the artemisia's rule of silver leaves and no-account flowers. This tall, handsome plant is also known as almond- or hawthorn-scented mugwort. A hardy Chinese native, it has slightly arching but self-supporting 6-foot-tall stems that are dressed top to toe with dark green lobed leaves, and its feathery, branching panicles are packed with small but abundant milk-white (hence *lacti-flora*) flowers. After several seasons, a single plant makes a striking, tall accent behind dark red or pink phlox, with daylilies or helenium of any hue or all on its own against a backdrop of evergreens or shrubs. Fertile, moist loam ensures robust growth and keeps foliage from turning yellow. Otherwise, the "milky mugwort," as I translate the Latin, grows itself. Cut this perennial back in late fall, or you will have a mess of smashed stems to cope with come spring. And if you need another plant or two, slice away divisions from the outer edges of an established clump in spring without lifting the parent plant.

Fairly quick from seed at the start, *Echinops ritro*, or its improved form 'Taplow Blue,' sometimes crops up in nurseries. However you start it, your original plants will likely spawn stripling thistles from their own hardy seeds. In very fertile, damp ground, echinops grow lush and sappy and may need some support.

Showy Stonecrop
(*Sedum spectabile*)

Bloom: August-frost
Height: 2½ feet
Color: pink
Needs: full sun

If I could grow just a dozen perennials, *Sedum spectabile* would be among them. Neither spectacular nor flamboyantly colored, the showy stonecrop is nevertheless a hard-working and dependable plant that maintains (with not a bit of attention) a neat and steady show of succulent gray-green foliage the season through, all the while masking fading bulb leaves or screening transient Oriental poppies behind. Its late and enduring flowering is decidedly welcome and serves to keep a border lively during the season of frosts, farewells and general seediness. The 2½-foot showy stonecrop, grande dame of a genus of succulents that includes a number of smaller species useful for edgings or sunny rock gardens, thrives unattended in any soil short of soggy, either in full sun or shaded for a few hours a day.

Late August sees the dome of broccoli-like buds begin to shade from pale green to mauve-pink as the massed, starry flowers open, drawing hungry honeybees and passing butterflies. The flower heads deepen in color during September and finally mellow to rusty brown in harmony with the shades of fall. Frost leaves this tough plant unscathed, however. Upright, self-supporting and symmetrical in its growth, showy stonecrop is a calm and orderly presence among perennials that are prone to sprawl or topple.

Fine as a specimen plant, this perennial is even more effective in groups of three, five or more, set toward the middle of a mixed border. Nursery plants—these will likely be the cultivars 'Brilliant,' 'Autumn Joy' or 'Meteor'—or plants from a neighbor's garden are the best way to introduce the showy stonecrop. In spring, established clumps can be split down to the last shoot if neces-